K-Culture로 배우는 시사영어

김경석 지음

신아사

K-ARTS K-DRAMA K-FOOD K-POP K-MOVIE K-FASHION K-BEAUTY

김경석

(현) 경기대학교 영어영문학과 교수
고려대학교 영어교육과 학사
University of Illinois at Urbana-Champaign 영어교육학 석사
University of Pennsylvania 교육언어학 박사

한국영어교육학회 부회장
대학수학능력시험 출제위원
중등교사 임용시험 출제위원
외무고시 2차 시험 출제위원
기술고시, 지방고시 시험위원
경찰대학교 1차 시험 출제위원
국비유학생 선발 1차 시험 출제위원
국가직 7급 공채시험 출제위원
국가직 9급 공채시험 출제위원
지방직 7급 공채시험 출제위원
지방직 9급 공채시험 출제위원
경찰공무원 채용시험 출제위원
부산시 공무원 임용시험 출제위원
경기도 지방공무원 임용시험 출제위원
국가영어능력시험 출제위원

K-Culture로 배우는 시사영어

초판 1쇄 발행 _ 2022년 4월 11일

저　자 · 김 경 석
발행인 · 정 현 걸
발　행 · 신 아 사
인　쇄 · 토탈프로세스
주　소 · 서울특별시 은평구 통일로 59길 4 (2층)
전　화 · (02) 382-6411　팩스 · (02) 382-6401
홈페이지 · www.shinasa.co.kr
E-mail · shinasa@daum.net
출판등록 · 1956년 1월 5일 (제 9-52호)

ISBN 979-11-91158-90-8 (93740)

정가 18,000원

이 도서는 2020학년도 경기대학교 연구년 수혜로 연구되었음.

머리말

어떤 분야를 새로이 또는 지속적으로 학습할 때 흥미로운 내용은 학습의 효율을 높이는데 있어 매우 중요한 요소로 작용한다. 'K-Culture로 배우는 시사영어'는 우리나라의 문화 중에서 세대를 초월해서 좋아하고 흥미를 가지고 있으며, 해외에서 또한 많은 인기를 누리고 있는 세부 문화들에 대한 외국인들의 반응을 해외 영어 미디어매체에서 소개하는 내용을 다루고 있다. 해외에서 큰 인기와 더불어 경제적으로도 우리나라에 많은 이득을 안겨주고 있는 K-Drama, K-Pop, K-Movie, K-Food, K-Beauty 그리고 서서히 그 입지를 탄탄히 다져나가고 있는 K-Fashion과 K-Arts에 이르기까지 K-Culture에 대한 다양한 현상들을 다루고 있다. 그러한 현상들을 정확하고 깊이 이해하기 위해서 필요한 전문 시사용어에 대한 설명과 폭 넓은 배경 정보를 아울러 제시하고 있다. 또한 언어 학습의 측면에서는 글을 정확히 이해하는데 필요한 문법, 어휘적인 설명을 포함하고 있다. 덧붙여 글의 내용을 잘 이해했는지 확인해 볼 수 있는 다양한 연습 문제들을 답과 함께 제시하고 있어 스스로 공부하는 경우에 보탬을 주고자 하였다. 아무쪼록 이 책이 우리에게 너무나 친숙하고 해외에서 인기 있는 문화 현상들을 영어 매체에서 전달하는 방법과 전문 시사 표현을 익히는데 있어 많은 도움이 되었으면 하는 바람을 가져본다.

Contents

Chapter I

K-Drama

Korean TV dramas find a huge audience in India

South Korean television series are having surprising successes on streaming services in India. The phenomenon has even prompted many Indians to learn Korean. Scherezade Shroff spent the initial weeks of India's 2020 coronavirus lockdown **binge-watching** all her favorite movies and shows online. But nothing could have prepared her for the world she entered after clicking on the Netflix icon for *Crash Landing on You*, a hugely popular South Korean television series.

"I had almost **run out of things to watch** when my best friend pushed me to give this show a shot. This was my initiation into the K-drama world," Shroff, a popular beauty and lifestyle YouTuber in India, told **DW**. *Crash Landing on You* was released in December 2019, but it wasn't until March 2020 that it became a cultural phenomenon in India—a development that not many could have anticipated. The show is about a paragliding **mishap** that "drops a South Korean heiress in North Korea, and into the life of an army officer, who decides he will help her hide."

Hyun Bin Philippine Fan Club meeting. source: www.happyrichtv.com

* binge-watch: 몰아서 보다(=watch multiple episodes of a TV show in one sitting)
* run out of things to watch: 시청할 만한 것이 없다
* DW: a global English-language news and information program from German public international broadcaster Deutsche Welle
* mishap: 불운한 사고(=unfortunate accident)

Over the past decade, Korean dramas and music—better known as K-pop have driven a global phenomenon sometimes called the "Korean wave." In India, the subculture commanded a **niche** audience. Students and young people from the country's northeastern states felt inspired by the romantic storylines, the cuisine, as well as the fashion choices of the **star-studded casts**.

Prior to the rise of streaming services such as Netflix and Amazon Prime, there were limited options available to view Korean dramas. The process typically involved trying to access a number of **shady** websites and waiting for a single episode to **buffer**—only to be confronted with substandard subtitles. The game changed with Netflix's latest push to bring South Korean content to the world. Now, a wider range of shows can be easily accessed by a larger audience.

* niche: 틈새
* star-studded cast: 화려한 출연진
* shady: 떳떳하지 못한, 수상한(=suspicious, crooked)
* buffer: 업로드하다

Focus on Grammar

◈ only to+verb

The process typically involved trying to access a number of shady websites and waiting for a single episode to buffer—*only to be* confronted with substandard subtitles.

'only to+verb' 표현은 앞에서 언급된 일의 결과가 실망스럽게도 '결국 ~ 하다'는 뜻을 지니고 있다. 흔히 말하는 'to 부정사'의 '결과적 용법'이다. 위 문장은, 여러 떳떳하지 못한 website를 통해서 k-drama에 접근하고 한 편의 에피소드를 업로드받기 위해서 많은 시간을 기다리면 마침내 수준 이하의 자막을 접하게 된다는 의미이다.

- They built the business from nothing only to lose it.
- A customer took a washing machine in for repair, only to be told it needed replacing.

During the coronavirus lockdown, *Crash Landing on You* beat several domestic hits and made it to Netflix's top 10 in India. "I have watched a number of regional shows in the past, but the difference here is that you can't just watch one Korean show and stop there. It takes you in: the culture, the lifestyle, the similarities it bears to our values in India, and finally, the dreaminess of it all," Shroff said. Shroff soon noticed that her Instagram followers were having conversations about K-dramas under her posts. So she decided to set up a Facebook group for fans.

Sherry's K-Drama Club is a Facebook group for people who want to share Korean film and series recommendations, give reviews, or simply **gush** over celebrities such as Lee Min-ho or Park Seo-joon.

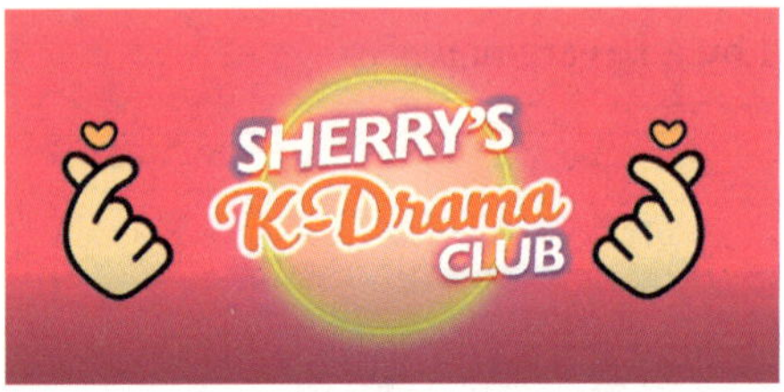

source: Sherry Shroff's Facebook

＊ gush: 쏟아내다(=express oneself extravagantly or emotionally; talk effusively)

"Focus on Terminology"

◈ words associated with celebrities

bigwig	a prominent or significant person
dignitary	an important or influential person
has-been	one that is no longer famous, popular, or successful
heartthrob	a person who is the object of popular romantic desire
infamy	extremely bad reputation or strong condemnation as the result of a shameful, criminal, or outrageous act
kahuna	an important person
luminary	one who inspires others or achieves eminence in a field
panjandrum	an important or influential person
pillar	a person who reliably provides essential support
standout	a person that is clearly superior to others

The group is comprised of people who have been watching Korean dramas for over 10 years when they weren't as easily available, as well as newcomers who watched their first K-drama during the lockdown. Some have watched more than 300 shows, while others are just wrapping up their first series. "It is a judgment-free space to talk about anything related to K-dramas—things we like, things that didn't work for us, issues like the importance of family or even sexism," Shroff said.

According to the YouTuber, K-drama is not just entertainment that you consume with your eyes and ears. When viewers watch a Korean show, they want to eat the food the characters are eating, they want to drink the drinks along with the **protagonist**.

* protagonist: 주인공(=the leading character of a drama or other literary work)

"Focus on Terminology"

◈ K-drama의 인기를 보여주는 media headlines in India

- India's romance with Korean-dramas gives way to K-craze among desi fans — The Indian Times
  * desi: local
- The Irresistible Pull Of Korean Dramas — www.outlook.com
- India's unstoppable hallyu: Why K-dramas matter — The Hindu
- Why are Indians head-over-heels in love with Korean dramas? — The Indian Express
- Korean Drama Heroes That Every Indian Has Fallen in Love With — The Sakshi Post
- Who is Anupam Tripathi? Here's all you need to know about the Indian actor who plays a Pakistani in the Korean series 'Squid Game' — The Times of India
- Why Indians are fascinated by K-dramas — The India Today
- South Koreans decode the rising global popularity of K-dramas — The Indian Express
- SHINee's Minho confirmed to appear in upcoming thriller drama 'Goosebumps' — The Times of India

"It is packaged as a deep dive into the culture as a whole," Shroff said. "The recall value is strong because there are recurring elements across dramas—the ramyun (Korean spicy noodles), tteokbokki (spicy rice cakes), mandu (dumplings) and soju (alcohol)." This has led to an increased demand for popular Korean food items across India.

an asian food store in Gurgaon, northern India. source: www.dw.com

"We have seen a sharp increase in the number of Indian customers over the past year," Subhash Kukreja, who owns a specialty store that **caters to** East Asian food in India's northern city of Gurgaon, told DW. Standing in front of a wall stocked with dozens of different ramyun brands and flavours, he said: "Korean spicy noodles are a favorite with our local customers."

* cater to: ~의 필요에 응하다, ~를 충족시키다

◇ 위 글의 문맥에 맞는 각 단어의 정의를 적절한 표현으로 채워 완성해봅시다.

1. Dive — To become suddenly and enthusiastically ____________ in something, as in eating food
2. Recall — The act of bringing back from ____________
3. Specialty — Meeting ____________ tastes or needs
4. Stock — To have or keep a ____________ of a particular product available for sale
5. Flavour — The distinctive ____________ of a food or drink

Shroff has been watching Korean shows for nearly a year and says everyday Korean words are now a part of her vocabulary. Interest in learning the Korean language has seen an **uptick** in India as the popularity of Korean pop culture surges. Some people are taking the extra step to learn the language by enrolling in professional programs or using apps.

The New Delhi-based Korean Cultural Centre India (KCCI), an **offshoot** of the South Korean embassy, runs numerous courses for people who want to learn the language. In response to **burgeoning** demand, the centre decided to host an online "Korean Language Hobby Class."

The speed of enrollments was overwhelming. In under two minutes, 600 people had registered for the class, forcing the center to close the registration. "Korean language has been solidified by India's New Education Policy in 2020 as a recommended foreign language," Hwang Il-yong, the director of KCCI, said in a press release.

* uptick: 약간의 증가(=a slight increase) ↔ downtick
* offshoot: 부서(=branch)
* burgeon: 급증하다(=grow or develop rapidly)

◇ 빈 칸에 들어갈 단어를 위 글에서 찾아 문장을 완성해봅시다.

1. Psychology began as a purely academic ____________ of natural philosophy.
2. The task won't feel so ____________ if you break it down into small, easy-to-accomplish steps.
3. Written exercises will expand your ____________ as well as your knowledge of grammatical structures.
4. The hard work has ____________ a dedicated fan base, but not without its consequences.
5. The lost incentives to give are likely to make a bigger difference than the small ____________ in economic growth expected from the new law.
6. Tonight she ____________ a party for 200 guests.

"We are in discussion with the CBSE (Central Board of Secondary Education) for the best ways to expand Korean language education in Indian schools in 2021," Hwang said. The organisation is also setting up both online and face-to-face courses in collaboration with the Korean-language King Sejong Institutes located in major cities in India.

Korean Cultural Centre in New Delhi. source: https://india.korean-culture.org

As Korean music and dramas make their ways into hundreds and thousands of homes throughout India—a country with a population of over 1 billion people—the Korean wave may have just hit one of the largest potential market jackpots in the world.

< King Sejong Institutes Worldwide >

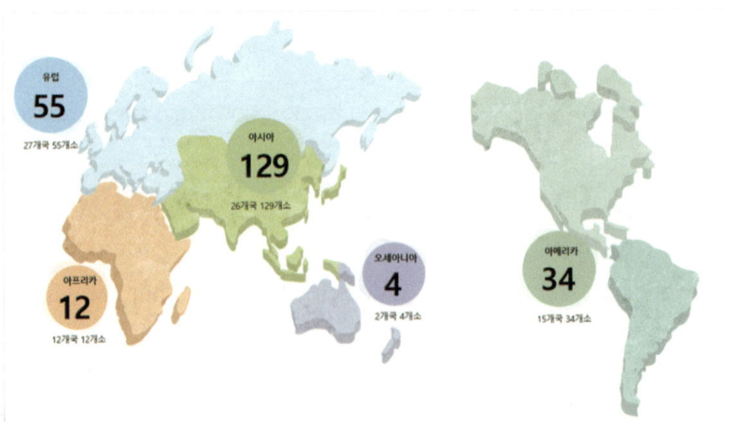

234 Institutes (8 in India) as of June, 2021. source: www.korea.net

Crash Landing On You (CLOY) 시청 후기

⦿ This drama was just perfect ♥ unlike other dramas where the whole plot revolves just around the lead roles. In CLOY every character had a significance be it his fellow army men or their wives and the chemistry of the second lead couple was also fierce. This drama was an emotional roller coaster. Experiencing a whole different life in North Korea and being astonished by the luxury of South Korea etc was just fab 😍😍 This drama was not even 1% cliche. CLOY and DOTS are one of the best dramas of this decade 😍😍😍 lots of love from india

* DOTS: Descendants of the Sun (태양의 후예)

⦿ Am I the only one who fell into major depression after this show ended? Like, I genuinely cannot move on. I'm so depressed and all I think about is the couple. I'm so sad 😭😭😭

⦿ I've watched exactly 44 kdramas now, and out of all the actors and characters I've watched and fell in love with, Captain Ri is the best of the bests. He's too perfect. And the chemistry of Hyun Bin and Son Ye Jin is unmatched! Out of all the dramas I've watched with great chemistry between the actors, they have the most natural chemistry.

⦿ This is the best K drama I've ever seen. All the ingredients are here, comedy, suspense, action and great love story. The main and supporting casts did their role superbly!!!!! The kissing scenes of Binjin were decently done yet the viewers could feel the great love they have for each other!!! The best Kdrama of all time!!!! This is the reason why CLOY is a phenomenal success globally!!!

* Binjin: Hyun Bin & Son Ye Jin

⦿ The worst thing I did was to watch CLOY as my first K Drama. Now none of the series can match its standards.

⦿ Every time I see Jeong Hyeok on the motorcycle without his helmet when he's rescuing Seri, my heart just flutters.

1. 다음의 단어들을 사용하여 빈 칸을 채워봅시다.

beloved sizzling slated delight adaptation abilities

While there is still no news about a second season of mega hit K-drama *Crash Landing On You*, fans of the cross-border romance will be happy to know that it is coming back in the form of a musical. Studio Dragon, the media firm which produced the drama, is working with two production companies, T2N Media and Pop Music, on the musical adaptation, __________ to be staged in Seoul in the middle of next year. Casting for the leads is reportedly about to start, although it is not known if the __________ original stars, Hyun Bin and Son Ye-jin, will be involved or if they have any singing __________. In the drama series, the character played by Hyun was not only a North Korean soldier, he was also a concert pianist, so a musical __________ seems like a natural progression. The chemistry between the two leads was so __________ that it spilled over to real life. Hyun and Son confirmed earlier this year that they were dating, much to the __________ of the fans who have dubbed the union #BinJin on social media.

2. 괄호 안 단어를 활용하여 적절한 표현으로 빈 칸을 채워봅시다.

a. CLOY catapulted Hyun Bin to ____________ (soar) popularity.

b. Fans of South Korean TV series are ardently waiting for *Crash Landing on You* Season 2's renewal and premiere since Season 1 ____________ (drop) its finale in mid-February 2020.

c. With input from real North Korean defectors, CLOY gives you a glimpse into what life in the hermit country might be like, while ____________ (explore) the differences and similarities between the two countries.

d. Korean actress Son Ye-jin, who starred in "Crash Landing on You," has been ____________ (cast) in a new drama. It was announced that Son Ye-jin has agreed to star in the drama "Thirty Nine."

Review: "Itaewon Class" Is a Story About Second Chances and Reaching For Your Dreams

Park Seo-joon stars in a new Korean drama, *Itaewon Class*, based on an **eponymous** webtoon. For those looking for a light-hearted Korean drama that's not too heavy on the romance side, look no further. *Itaewon Class* combines **snazzy** visuals, a fun ensemble cast, and a storyline that you might need tissues for—either from laughter or sadness.

Not Your Typical Revenge Plot

Itaewon Class follows Park Sae-ro-yi (Park Seo-joon), a kind-hearted boy who dreams of becoming a police officer. His teachers describe Park as socially **inept** because he doesn't interact much with other people, much less have friends. This worries his father (Park Sung-yeol), an employee at a large food corporation called *Jangga*. Park's kind-hearted nature turns on him as he saves a classmate from being bullied by Jang Geun Won (Ahn Bo-hyun). Little does he know, Jang's father is the CEO of *Jangga*. Park's school expels him, and *Jangga* fires his father. Adding to Park's miseries, an accident happens, leaving Park an orphan. He receives prison time for assaulting Jang, killing his dream of becoming a police officer. Park swears revenge on *Jangga*—by continuing his father's dreams of starting a business.

source: www.artstation.com

* eponymous: 작품명과 동일한 이름의
* snazzy: 멋진(=fashionable, flashy, stylish)
* inept: 서투른(=incompetent, clumsy)

It's not new to see revenge to play a role in the plot of Korean dramas. For some Korean drama characters, revenge is the driving force and ***raison d'etre***.

A Second Chance at Life for Outcasts

It's easy to say that *Itaewon Class* is a revenge story, but it's not. Instead, it's a story about second chances. Despite not being able to become a policeman, Park continues to live by principles that his father **instilled** in him. After leaving prison, Park starts a pub called *DanBam*. The *DanBam* crew are all, by nature, social outcasts like Park. Cho Yi-seo (Kim Da-mi), an influencer and social blogger is described as a sociopath by her classmates; Jang Geun-soo (Kim Dong-hee), an illegitimate son of *Jangga*'s CEO; Choi Seung-kwon (Ryoo Kyung-soo), a fellow ex-convict; the transgendered Ma Hyun-yi (Lee Joo-young); Tony Kim (Chris Lyon), an African-Korean "foreigner"; and Oh Soo-a (Kwon Nara), an orphan. *DanBam* is home to all these characters who are **cast** aside by society, whether it's because of social status, appearance, or sexuality.

* raison d'etre: 존재의 이유(=reason or justification for existing)
* instill: 주입시키다(=inculcate, infuse)
* cast: 던지다(=throw, hurl). cf. 현재-과거-과거분사형이 동일

이태원클래스 촬영지, 단밤. 사진: 김경석

Ex-convicts face a lot of discrimination in South Korea, and often find it hard to look for a job after getting out of prison. South Korea also rarely discusses **LGBTQ** issues. Transgender people and sexual minorities are still treated as if they're invisible. Meanwhile, biracial people like Tony Kim are labeled as "foreigners" in the country despite being part Korean—that actually happened in the drama as well.

Like Park's story, *Itaewon Class* follows these characters as they receive a second chance at life, whether it's small or big. It tells us that we can always start over, somewhere, and most importantly, with someone.

Small Steps Toward Your Dreams
Itaewon Class also tells us that there's no easy way to achieve our dreams. We have to take small steps. It might be bold of Park to think that his small-time pub can go against the largest food corporation in the country, but it also goes to show us how determined he is to follow his dreams. Despite his dark and sad past, Park doesn't **wallow** in pity at being an orphan or an ex-convict; instead, he looks forward to the future, and most importantly, doesn't lose sight of the lessons his father taught him.

* LGBTQ: lesbian, gay, bisexual, transgender, queer 또는 questioning
* wallow: 빠져있다(=indulge), 뒹굴다

Focus on Grammar

◆ Instead

... *instead*, he looks forward to the future, and most importantly, doesn't lose sight of the lessons his father taught him.

목적어를 필요로 하는 'instead of'와는 달리 instead는 부사로서 목적어를 필요로 하지 않으며 문장내에서 위치가 자유롭다.

- We left our car at home and used the train *instead*.
- The money spent on the project could *instead* have been used on buying more computers.

Fans of Park Seo-joon will definitely enjoy *Itaewon Class* as it further reinforces his versatility as an actor. We've seen him become the second lead in *Kill Me, Heal Me*, a **swoon-worthy** lead actor in other romantic comedies such as *Fight For My Way* and *What's Wrong With Secretary Kim* or in more serious roles such as such in the movie, *Divine Fury*.

Netizens raised some eyebrows at the fact that in the flashbacks, Park played his younger self despite a 9 year time difference. With even the same **buzz cut**, this casting choice didn't seem that believable. But had someone else played the younger Park, the same emotions of grief, anger, and hope would not have been portrayed as effectively as when Park did it himself.

* swoon-worthy: 황홀해 할만한

* buzz cut: 짧게 깍은 머리

Focus on Grammar

◆ 가정법 과거완료와 도치

But <u>*had someone else played*</u> the younger Park, the same emotions of grief, anger, and hope would not have been portrayed as effectively as when Park did it himself.

가정법 과거완료 구문인 'If 주어 + had + pp, 주어 + 조동사 과거형 + have + pp' 순서에서 위 예시 문장처럼 If절에 도치를 적용하면 if를 생략한다; But if someone else had played > But had someone else played

이와 같은 도치와 if의 생략은 가정법의 다른 시제에도 적용할 수 있다.

a. 가정법 과거 문장에서의 도치: If I were a bird, I could reach up there. > Were I a bird, I could reach up there.

b. 가정법 미래 문장에서의 도치: If you should change your mind, please give a call. > Should you change your mind, please give me a call.

c. 가정법 과거완료 문장에서의 도치: If I had known what you had in your mind, I would not have supported you. > Had I known what you had in your mind, I would not have supported you.

Newcomer Kim Da-mi, who gave an impressive performance as the main female lead in *The Witch: Part 1. The Subversion*, will also delight Korean drama viewers with her **no-fuss-given** attitude. Despite her debut small-screen role, she rises up to the challenge alongside her fellow actors.

source: www.wellgousa.com

However, the biggest treat for audiences is the chemistry between all the members of the *DanBam* crew. Anyone looking for a good friendship drama will surely find this appealing.

Itaewon Class is unfortunately not **immune** to typical Korean drama **tropes**, but it more than **makes up for** that. Excellent visuals filled with vibrant colors bring Itaewon's nightlife to life. **Sprinkle** in a good soundtrack and you have a Korean drama worth your time. Coming from JTBC, known for its Korean dramas spiced with social commentaries, be sure to expect no less from *Itaewon Class*.

* no-fuss-given: 호들갑 떨지 않는, 느긋한
* immune: 영향을 받지 않는(=not affected), 자유로운(=free from)
* trope: 비유(=figurative sense)
* make up for: 보충하다, 보상하다
* sprinkle: ~ 속에 빠지다(=intersperse)

◇ 다음 표현과 같은 의미를 지닌 단어를 위 글에서 찾아봅시다.

1. flavored
2. alchemy
3. secure against
4. delight (n.)
5. regrettably
6. deserving

Itaewon Class (IC) 시청 후기

⦿ I just finished *Itaewon Class* and it has completely wrecked and enchanted me. This drama as a whole is superior.

⦿ This is the best kdrama I watched so far. PSJ hits me so hard that when he's angry I felt his rage, when he's sad I couldn't help but cry and when he's happy I really am overjoyed. Superb acting.

⦿ Their soundtrack is something that makes it hard for me to let go of this series. Every song is so beautiful. The character of Yi Seo is also very refreshing! I hope there would be more female characters like that, but most importantly Kim Dami did a magnificent job in portraying a sociopath brat. In the end, she still won our hearts.

⦿ I love everything!! I miss SeoDami soooo much! I'm having a hard IC withdrawal huhuh. I wish to see SeoDami in another series or movie. Their chemistry is insane even if they have limited romantic scene from the movie. One of PSJ's best drama ever, and KDM's performance was spectacular too!!♥♥♥

⦿ Just finished Itaewon Class and I must say that this is by far the best Kdrama I watched. IC will teach you that trust and loyalty matters more than money. Opportunity shouldn't control loyalty. Genuine relationships outweigh temporary, good times. IC tells us that surrounding yourself with the right people regardless of race, gender, appearance will inspire you to keep moving even when difficult times.

⦿ Because of this drama, whenever I see other dramas, they just look so trash, can't help 😂. The writings is very good and I think it's carefully planned too.

⦿ Yiseo is the real star of this drama❤❤started watching because of seojooni and ended up falling in love with dami❤❤

⦿ I need a special episode or a season 2 or a movie. Whatever it is, I don't mind. I just need more and more *Itaewon class* for the rest of my life, this is a masterpiece and also the best love story ever.

⦿ When I was watching *Itaewon class*, I had already said if Saeroyi didn't end up with Yiseo I'd throw my phone 😂😂😂 Thank God he did! and my phone is in one piece.

1. 다음의 단어들을 사용하여 빈 칸을 채워봅시다.

expand arm acclaimed synergy acquired meaning

According to *The Los Angeles Times*, JTBC Studios, the production company of *Itaewon Class*, is in talks to produce its English version with help from its newly __________ subsidiary Wiip. Wiip, which JTBC bought in June 2021, is a Hollywood-based production company that was originally owned by noted talent agency Creative Artists Agency. The production __________ is also known for its work on __________ television shows such as HBO's *Mare of Easttown*. "There is a great __________ for us entering into the Hollywood production market, producing in English, producing with American or international talents out there to __________ our business," said JTBC senior vice president Hong Jeong-in about the potential English remake of *Itaewon Class*. "There'll be instant __________."

2. 괄호 안 단어를 활용하여 적절한 표현으로 빈 칸을 채워봅시다.

a. ____________ (release) in 2020, *Itaewon Class* was widely regarded as one of the year's best South Korean shows.

b. Prior to *Itaewon Class*, Park Seo-joon was the male lead in a number of South Korean dramas, many of which being romantic comedies where his chemistry with the main female star ____________ (be) central to his performance.

c. While Park is recognized primarily for his TV projects, the actor ____________ (have) a successful career in the movie industry as well, with roles in *Be With You*, *The Divine Fury*, *Midnight Runners*, and more.

d. Park, who has crafted a big following in South Korea, stands at chance at also ____________ (become) big in the West when he makes his Hollywood debut in *The Marvels*.

e. It remains to ____________ (see) if he'll play an established Marvel Comics hero or villain, as the details of his role have yet to be disclosed.

Netflix's 'Kingdom' Is the Perfect Show to Binge If You Miss 'Game of Thrones'

The show begins with rumors of the death of the king of Joseon, who hasn't been seen outside the palace walls for more than a week. **Flyers appear tacked up** in Hanyang, announcing the king's death and calling for the immediate crowning of the prince, Lee Chang (Ju Ji-hoon). However, those inside the palace claim the king is not dead, merely sick, but his **affliction** has turned him into something monstrous.

Meanwhile, citizens in a small town in the southern province unknowingly **contract** the disease **ravaging** the king and die suddenly, but that night they all rise again as zombies, hungry for human flesh (as zombies tend to be).

source: www.mothership.sg

* flyers appear tacked up: (사극 드라마에서 볼 수 있는) 방(벽보)이 내걸리다. flyer의 요즘 뜻은 전단지(=flier, leaflet)
* affliction: 고통(=great suffering due to ill health)
* contract(v): 질병에 걸리다(=acquire, become affected by)
* ravage: 파괴하다, 황폐화 시키다

Focus on Vocabulary

◈ binge

원래는 음식과 관련하여 '(자기 통제를 못하고) ~에 빠지다(=be unrestrained in + food/drink)' 뜻으로 사용하였는데 그 의미가 나날이 확장되어 다양한 탐닉대상에 쓰이고 있다. 명사 표현으로 binge eating, binge drinking, binge watching, binge reading 등이 있으며, 형용사 표현으로 binge-worthy(빠질만한 가치가 있는)가 대표적이다: 예, The drama is truly binge-worthy.

The crown prince sets off from the palace to help the people in need, but when he discovers the truth of the disease, he teams up with a physician, a mysterious warrior, and his personal guard to fight the spread of the disease while also trying to stop a **coup** from overthrowing his claim to the throne back home.

Plus, the zombies in Kingdom are actually scary—mostly because they're quite different from the kind of zombies we're familiar with. For one thing, they can run, which inspires some truly frightening scenes of undead people **sprinting** through tall grass **at their prey**. They also go **dormant** during the daytime (for a reason that becomes very important by the first season's finale) when the sun is out and hide by **cramming** themselves in piles underneath houses and fallen trees and caves in the woods. I'm so unbelievably bored of zombies by now and even I loved this.

Kingdom 촬영지. 포천 비둘기 낭 폭포. source: www.pocheon.go.kr

* coup: coup d'état
* sprint: 전력질주하다(=move at full speed)
* at their prey: 먹잇감을 찾아(쫓아)
  └ predator: 포식자, 약탈자
  └ predate (v): 1. ~를 잡아먹다 2. ~ 보다 앞서다
  └ predatory pricing: 주변 경쟁자들을 제거할 목적으로 가격을 매우 낮게 책정하는 것
* dormant: 활동하지 않는(=inactive, latent)
* cram: 우겨넣다(=force or squeeze (something) into an insufficient space)

It's more than just a zombie show, though: at its core, Kingdom is much more interested in **picking apart** systems of power, and how stubbornness and an unwillingness to see the truth can lead to catastrophe. The first season of the show is all about the kingdom being unable to stop the outbreak of the disease. By the time the show picks up in Season 2, the zombies are coming closer and closer to the capitol, and those inside the palace are still **scheming** against the prince, with a few even attempting to try to control the undead **plague** to their advantage.

* pick apart: 문제점을 상세히 들여다보다
* scheme (v): 계획하다(=plan, plot, contrive)
* plague: 전염병(=epidemic, pandemic)

"Focus on Grammar"

◈ 미래시제

By the time the show picks[1] up in Season 2, the zombies are coming[2] closer and closer to the capitol.

이 문장에서 1, 2번 동사 표현 모두 미래를 의미 한다("앞으로 개봉할 킹덤 Season 2 에서는 좀비들이 수도(한양)로 더 가까이 다가올 것이다"). 시간을 나타내는 접속사가 이끄는 부사절에서는 미래 의미를 나타낼 때 현재 시제를 사용하는데, 이 문장에서 By the time이 그런 접속사 중의 하나이다. 'As soon as', 'as long as', 'now that' 또한 시간 접속사인데, 여기서 주의해야할 점은 접속사가 두 단어 이상 일 수 있음에 유의해야 한다. 2번째 'be + 동사ing' 표현의 경우, 현재 진행형을 의미하는 것이 아니라 미래를 의미한다. 'will + 동사' 'be going to + 동사' 등과 더불어 미래 의미를 나타내는 대표적인 표현 중 하나이다. 'be + 동사ing'는 미래에 일어날 일이 이미 어느 정도 확정된 경우에 주로 사용한다. 위 문장에는 Season 2의 내용이 이미 공개되었고 촬영하고 있는 상황이기 때문에 그런 표현을 사용하고 있다.

• By the time they are six weeks old, they are coming out of the nest.
• Dinner will be ready by the time you get back.
• By the time he is 40 years old, he will have all the possible titles.

Kingdom 시청 후기

I'm just impressed how creative Korean movies are. Just perfect acting, plots and cinematography. Originality is the best.

South Koreans know how to make things epic. I just finished this show 30 minutes ago and OMG it was freaking amazing. Cinematography, story line, the acting. Its action packed with twists and turns you least expect it. The writer is the same writer who wrote the unbelievable drama series "Signal". She is pure genius I tell you. The same director who filmed "The Tunnel" (loved that movie as well). I HIGHLY, HIGHLY recommend this to anyone.

I only discovered this show yesterday. Yeah, I know, shame on me. But I binged it like a mad man. It was just amazing, I'm in love with this show. So well done, I'm really impressed. Let's go for season 2. I'm beyond excited, it feels good.

I wonder if Koreans realise how much we enjoy their cinema. I'm a huge fan of theirs and they make far greater than hollyweird and all other Americans.

Three reasons why you should watch "Kingdom" 1. Zombies 2. Fancy Hats 3. Ju Ji Hoon

I love zombie movies and series. I've watched tons of them but I carry this one in my heart, it was amazing from start to end, such a shame it is not very famous in Italy.

I HONESTLY WATCH THIS 5 TIMES ALREADY AND WHENEVER I WATCH IT, IT STILL HIT DIFFERENT!!! KOREAN MAKES THE BEST ZOMBIE MOVIE CLAIM IT.

Joo ji hoon is born to play the role of every Korean prince.

Honestly, this show gives me chills from start to finish.

I really appreciate how much detail is put into the characters and how they drive the story, definitely not a typical zombies show, just when I thought the genre was running dry this show rehydrates it for me with its originality, bravo to the writer she's a genius 👍👍

Seen it and what a cliffhanger that was. As always, Korea never fails to do great shows and films.

1. 다음의 단어들을 사용하여 빈 칸을 채워봅시다.

benchmarked everyday expressed longevity spared emotional

"Kingdom" costume designer Kwon Yoo-jin says the team was looking for a balance between the magnificent and the mundane. "We wanted to emphasize the unique beauty, delicacy and colors of Korea," Kwon explains, "but at the same time, show the common people's __________ life filled with struggle and sweat." The capital city of Hanyang, current-day Seoul, served as the setting for much of the story, and no detail was __________. Visuals were inspired by authentic locations, including Gyeongbok Palace, the main royal Joseon stronghold. Colors, materials and textures, down to their glosses and reflections, were __________. For the queen's residence, Gyotaejeon Hall, interiors were built with several connecting chambers to convey her __________ depth and used colors from Sipjangsaeng, a decorative form of traditional Korean art illustrating 10 symbols of __________. By combining lucid fixtures and vivid hues, the life and vitality of the young woman were __________.

2. 괄호 안 단어를 활용하여 적절한 표현으로 빈 칸을 채워봅시다.

a. When Netflix's first South Korean original series, *Kingdom*, premiered in 2019, the horror series ____________ (be) met with positive reception.

b. *Kingdom* explores an appetite for power that ____________ (interlink) with an insatiable craving for flesh.

c. A physician ____________ (tend) to the ailing king cautions his assistant to avert his gaze from his ruler. The boy's curiosity reveals that the king has become a beast who snacks on human flesh.

d. Accused of treason, Lee Chang escapes with his loyal bodyguard to meet the physician and find out if his father indeed has smallpox or something ____________ (bad).

e. ____________ (starve) plays its part in spreading the plague beyond the capital.

'My Mister' and Its Story of Loneliness

With all the good K-dramas being released almost week after week, it's definitely hard to keep up with the new ones, as well as the already-completed ones that are sitting in your binge lists for the longest time. However, just like every binge-watcher out there, you're probably still on the lookout for more dramas to add to your never-ending lists. If that's the case, then we've **got your back**!

For this week's K-drama files, we put the spotlight on *My Mister* and why you should watch it!

The Story

My Mister follows a middle-aged man named Park Dong Hoon, who works as a middle-aged engineer married to the lawyer Kang Yoon Hee. Despite living a seemingly good life, he's unhappy, with two unemployed brothers relying on him, and a wife who's in a secret affair with his CEO Do Joon Young.

Things **take a turn** for him when he receives an unexpected bribe, and he learns that his co-worker, Lee Ji An, saw him. The young part-timer has an ill grandmother and is struggling with different part-time jobs to be able to pay their debt. Dong Hoon then gets entangled with her, all while trying to help his brothers, and getting caught between office rivalry.

나의 아저씨 촬영지. 인천 만석동.
source: www.naver.com

* get one's back: 도와주다, 지키다
* take a turn: 상황이 변하다(=change in condition/quality, especially suddenly)

The Cast

At the center of the story is Lee Sun Kyun, who plays Park Dong Hoon, an engineer living an unhappy life. You may know the 45-year-old actor for his roles in *Parasite* and *Coffee Prince*. IU plays Lee Ji An, a 20-something part-timer who struggles to pay for her debts while caring for her sick grandmother. The actress also starred in dramas *Dream High*, *Moon Lovers* and *Hotel Del Luna*. Joining the two leads are Park Ho San and Song Sae Byuk, who play Dong Hoon's brothers, Sang Hoon and Gi Hoon. Kim Young Min plays CEO Do Joon Young.

Watch it if you ...

... are looking for a K-drama that's unlike all the other dramas you've watched before. *My Mister* is far from the rom-com and lighthearted dramas you saw before. It's dark and it's heavy, with a bit of dark comedic moments in between.

The drama talks a lot about loneliness and the issues that come with being an adult in a competitive place such as Seoul. Though we don't live in Korea, I'm pretty sure that there will be moments where you will see yourself in one of the characters in the drama. It can be with Dong Hoon who's still unhappy despite living a "good life"; with Ji An and her struggle to keep herself **afloat**; or with Dong Hoon's brothers whose dreams have been crushed because ~life~.

* **afloat**: 곤경에서 벗어난(=free or out of difficulty, especially financial difficulty)

"Focus on Grammar"

◈ 문법보다는 의미를 선택

... or with Dong Hoon's brothers whose dreams have been crushed <u>*because ~life~*</u>.

접속사 because 다음에는 주어+동사를 포함하는 절을 사용해야 한다. 하지만 이 글에서는 '그들이 삶에서 겪은 시련'을 한 단어인 life로 응축하여 표현하고 있다.

Don't be **put off** with the episode's longer running time, too. It's worth taking your time with, and it feels like you go through every character's story and struggle with every episode that you watch.

My Mister is an emotional roller coaster of a story that every K-drama fan must see. It has a story that's full of heart and a talented **cast** that you'd want to **root for**. Besides, it didn't win Best Drama at the Baeksang Arts Awards for nothing, right?

* put off: 포기하다(=discard)
* root for: 응원하다(=show strong sympathy for)

"Focus on Vocabulary"

◆ cast

명사로서 cast는 다양한 뜻을 지니고 있는데, 이 글에서는 '출연자들(a group of actors in a movie or drama)'을 의미한다. 주요 명사 뜻으로 (낚싯줄, 주사위 등을) 던지기, 거푸집(mould), 행운(fortune), 예상(forecast), 유형(type), 경향(inclination) 등이다. 동사 '던지다'의 뜻으로 가장 친숙한 표현은 Caesar가 Rubicon강을 건널 때 남긴 명언을 들 수 있다: "The dice is cast."

나의 아저씨 촬영지. 서울시 용산 백빈건널목. 사진: 김경석

My Mister 시청 후기

⊙ This is one of the very few TV series that I wanted to get a hard copy of it in DVD or Blue Ray so I can treasure it for the rest of my life. I can't wait to watch it a second time after I binged it on Netflix in two days.

⊙ Incomparable!! Complex characters intertwined to form a beautiful story. It is not a love story, but you can feel a different kind of love with a deeper meaning. I love the character of Dong hoon. He is a total package of a real gentleman. On the other hand, Ji-an as a loving granddaughter, tough and fierce in her battle to live. Watching this film was a roller coaster of emotions. A lot of reference to reflect on life, living and loving. Even the sounds of their deep breaths, sounds of their steps and the looks in their eyes tell a story. And every intense scene cut like a knife that leaves you breathless. I needed to rest my mind after watching this film ... in a good way. It made me think of my life in the past, my present and the choices in the future. ❤ This film deserves an international recognition! 👏👏👏

⊙ I just finished watching this show. At first I only watched this after watching IU's *Hotel Del Luna*. I wanna watch more of her work. But after watching episode 1, I totally fall in love with the story. Every bit of this drama is so great. It makes you think, reflect and feel your deepest emotion. Part of me can relate to every character. It's painful yet healing. It kinda gives that faith to human kindness. That there are still genuinely kind people in this cruel world.

⊙ My little sister summarized this drama the best IMHO. This one was the very depressing story and yet gave you the greatest healing inside.

* IMHO: In My Humble Opinion

⊙ This drama was soo good even sometimes the scene without any dialogue can hold many feelings. I don't know how they can do that. The political conflict also not bored me. The love here is soo mature not "romance love" things. But love for other human being. Watching this drama is like you are home drinking a warm soup after a hard cold day if you get what I mean.

1. 다음의 단어들을 사용하여 빈 칸을 채워봅시다.

drag temp company astounding cast ailing

A truly unique Korean drama, *My Mister* tells the story of a cold woman who has suffered many hardships in her life, who finds sympathy and comfort in the __________ of three brothers who are healing from their own trauma. The series is deeply profound and addresses a number of serious topics. The __________ is led by Lee Ji-eun, also known by her stage name IU, who plays Lee Ji-an, a woman who will do anything to support her __________ grandmother. She encounters the middle brother, Park Dong-hoon (Lee Sun-kyun), when she is hired as a __________ worker at his company. A coworker instructs her to find out Dong-hoon's secrets, but soon enough she's falling for the man, who seems to understand more about her than anyone she's ever met. Although it's definitely a slow-moving story, the __________ acting and remarkably written characters will __________ you in and keep you enthralled until the last episode. *My Mister* is a must-watch, especially if you are a fan of serious dramas.

2. 괄호 안 단어를 활용하여 적절한 표현으로 빈 칸을 채워봅시다.

a. Idols are often criticized for being one-dimensional actors, but one singer who subverts this expectation is IU, who has been steadily ____________ (gain) popularity as a distinguished actress.

b. IU takes charge of the role of a strong, cold woman in ____________ (finance) struggle and must learn to trust other people in order to heal her past scars.

c. *My Mister* is a very ____________ (restrain) drama with characters who bear great trauma underneath the surface.

d. ____________ (assure) writing, tender directing, and outstanding performances from the cast all come together to make *My Mister* an absorbing watch that feels organic, real and raw.

한국 드라마의 영어 제목

외국에 드라마를 수출할 때 제목을 글자 그대로 번역하는 경우도 있지만, 때론 전혀 다른 영어 제목을 사용하는 경우도 있다. 다음은 각각 어떤 드라마의 제목인지 알아 맞혀봅시다.

영어 제목	방영 연도	주연 배우	우리말 제목
Dr. Romantic	2016	한석규, 서현진, 유현석	
Innocent Defendant	2017	지성, 엄기준, 권유리	
Prison Playbook	2018	박해수, 정경호, 정수정	
100 Days My Prince	2018	도경수, 남지현, 조성하	
When the Camellia Blooms	2019	공효진, 강하늘, 김지석	
The Fiery Priest	2019	김남길, 이하늬, 김성균	
It's Okay Not to Be Okay	2020	서예지, 김수현, 곽동연	
The World of the Married	2020	김희애, 박해준, 한소희	
Taxi Driver	2021	이제훈, 이솜, 표예진	
	2017	남궁민, 이준호, 남상미	김과장
	2017	박서준, 김지원, 송하윤	쌈 마이웨이
	2019	이나영, 이종석, 정유진	로맨스는 별책부록
	2019	여진구, 이세영, 김상경	왕이 된 남자
	2020	조정석, 전미도, 유연석	슬기로운 의사생활
	2020	김서형, 염정아, 오나라	SKY 캐슬
	2020	신혜선, 김정현, 나인후	철인왕후
	2021	조병규, 김세정, 유준상	경이로운 소문
	2021	신민아, 김선호	갯마을 차차차

< Famous Quotes About Drama >

Q Drama starts where logic ends. — Ram Charan

Q There are always going to be hospital dramas because if you're sitting in an emergency room for two hours, I guarantee you that you are going to see something that makes you gasp. That's where drama comes from. — Rocky Carroll

Q The human mind is a dramatic structure in itself and our society is absolutely saturated with drama. — Edward Bond

Q People talk worse about people than they talk good about people, because a lot of people like drama. — Hilary Duff

Q Heroes in drama are people who try hard to reach a virtuous ideal. And whether they succeed or fail really doesn't matter—it's the trying that counts. — Aaron Sorkin

Q I really hate drama. It's draining; it's mentally draining. It's a waste of time. — Carli Lloyd

Q It's hard enough to write a good drama, it's much harder to write a good comedy, and it's hardest of all to write a drama with comedy. Which is what life is. — Jack Lemmon

Q Truth in drama is forever elusive. You never quite find it, but the search for it is compulsive. The search is clearly what drives the endeavour. The search is your task. — Harold Pinter

Q Drama can be an addiction. It's so, so sneaky. Jealousy—all of those things can really send you in a lot of different crazy directions. — Christian Slater

Q I've never gotten hired for drama because I'm a good improviser. I don't think people who write drama scripts want you playing with them as much. — Matt Walsh

Q Drama's not safe and it's not pretty and it's not kind. People expect the basic template of television drama where there might be naughty villains, but everyone ends up having a nice cup of tea. You've got to do big moral choices and show the terrible things people do in terrible situations. Drama is failing if it doesn't do that. — Russell Davies

Cross-word Puzzle

ACROSS

2. stylish in a way that attracts attention
4. to store data
5. having or showing no skill
7. one of the main characters in a story or a play
10. to teach and impress by frequent repetitions
11. alive but not active
14. an epidemic disease that causes high mortality
15. a figurative use

DOWN

1. to begin to increase rapidly
2. to move at full speed
3. something that makes you suffer
6. a small increase
8. to indulge oneself in emotion
9. questionable as to honesty
12. to cause extensive damage to
13. to pour out suddenly in large amounts

Chapter II

K-POP

Can South Korea's Pop Superstars Sell Everything?

Fast food and a soft drink. It's a standard takeaway order worldwide. This summer in South East Asia, this **prosaic** combo was sprinkled with pop **stardust**. Korean style.

The world's biggest boy and girl bands, BTS and Blackpink, contracted their immense selling power to two of the planet's largest brands, McDonald's and Pepsi. Two campaigns for fried chicken meals and a low-sugar soda **supercharged** sales and social media engagement from Kuala Lumpur to Manila to Hanoi.

The response to the BTS-McDonald's tie-up was dramatic. "When two giants collide, chaos ensues," noted Campaign Asia. In Indonesia, surging demand saw some outlets temporarily postpone orders. "Don't overcrowd. There's enough BTS meals for everyone," McDonald's in Malaysia pleaded on social media.

Meanwhile, TV stations region-wide replayed Blackpink's Pepsi Black ads for weeks, with the tagline "No sugar, no regrets" adapted in different markets. In Malaysia, for example, it became, "Rasa Hebat, Tanpa Kalori"—great taste, no calories.

Blackpink concert in Malaysia source: www.yljack.com

* prosaic: 평범한(=ordinary, dull, commonplace)
* stardust: 매혹적인 감성(=a magical or charismatic quality or feeling)
* supercharge: (판매를) 촉진시키다

The promotional results confirmed two trends. Firstly, the power in brand communications resides with visual content leaders. Secondly, star power often trumps innovation. Neither McDonald's nor Pepsi launched dazzling new products. Instead, they repackaged standard offerings and bathed in the marketing **glitz** that is K-Pop.

Confirming why McDonald's chose BTS, the Chief Marketing Officer for Malaysia, said simply: "This band is truly a global phenomenon with a fanbase that knows no borders."

Pepsi, which hired Blackpink as its Asia Pacific brand ambassadors, was equally concise. "Blackpink perpetuates a uniquely youthful attitude and zest for life that inspires fans to **emulate** their idols."

The Making of Megastars

It's hard to overstate how popular each band is in South East Asia. For aspirational young consumers, BTS and Blackpink embody the intrinsic sense of desire fortifying the Korean Wave of TV, beauty and pop culture. A **beguiling** mix of glamour, celebrity and sex appeal ensures **idolatry**. The illusory world of social media assumes they are personally accessible. This powerful mix makes them **coveted** influencers for blue-chip brands.

* glitz: 화려함(=flashiness), 호화로움
* emulate: 모방하다(=imitate, copy, follow)
* beguiling: 매력적인(=fascinating, attractive, alluring)
* coveted: 갈망하는(=sought-after)

"Focus on Vocabulary"

◈ suffix (접미사) -latry

A beguiling mix of glamour, celebrity and sex appeal ensures *idolatry*.

'우상 숭배' 뜻을 지닌 idolatry는 그리스어에서 '이미지'를 뜻하는 eidōlon에 '숭배'의 뜻을 지닌 접미사 -latreia를 더한 eidōlolatreia에서 유래한다. Old French에서는 idolatrie로 쓰이다가 중세 영어에 들어서 idolatry를 사용하기 시작하였다. 다른 예시 단어로 '마귀(귀신) 숭배'를 뜻하는 demonolatry를 들 수 있다.

None of this occurred by chance. The formulas for global pop domination were created by two ambitious Seoul talent agencies.

BTS was formed and **fast-tracked** by Big Hit Entertainment, whose website boasts of "unmatched structured training" for new artists. Although promoted by YG Entertainment as Korean stars, Blackpink's members share diverse backgrounds, including New Zealand. The agency candidly says it "trains artists to lead the global market."

The commercial minds behind both bands produce and sell regularly refreshed lines of merchandise, special edition videos and playlists, which keep them top-of-mind **while global tours are impossible**. BTS has taken this further by opening pop-up concept stores selling themed lifestyle products in prime city locations in Indonesia, Malaysia, Philippines and Thailand.

And of course, band members **adroitly** switch into brand ambassadorial mode. Much of their appeal to brands resides in their **media ubiquity**, and the multiple roles they fulfil for their fans. As *Vogue Business* recently stated: "K-pop singers won't just wear brands on the red carpet but in a plethora of other ways, from making music, doing TV shows and filming movies to dancing and modelling."

* fast-track: 빠르게 성공하다
* while global tours are impossible: Covid-19 pandemic으로 인해서 공연이 불가능한 상황을 언급
* adroitly: 빠르고 능숙하게(=dexterously)

"Focus on Terminology"

◈ media ubiquity

다양한 매체에서 아주 흔하게 접할 수 있음을 의미한다. 대중들이 잘 접할 수 있도록 미디어 산업에서 여러 형태의 platform에 정보를 배포시키고 잘 유통되도록 하는 것을 spreadability라고 한다. on-line platforms에서 정보가 가장 활발하게 배포/유통되고 있는 요즘에는 흔히들 influencer라고 부르는 social media celebrity/social media personality들의 영향력이 급증하고 있다.

Taking K-Pop Onto a Grander Stage
Although their early successes were gleaned in Asia, both management teams targeted the US. Being able to sing and rap in English therefore proved a vital, and lucrative, skillset.

Blackpink has enjoyed musical collaborations with **A-List female performers**, such as Lady Gaga, Selena Gomez, Cardi B and Dua Lipa. These guaranteed regular radio play and video streaming, and showcased their Korean brand of **sassy** rap-pop to new fan bases. Concert performances **burnished** Blackpink's reputation. In 2019, the band's debut at the Coachella festival was live-streamed by YouTube on a giant screen in New York's Times Square.

Blackpink's contract with smartphone maker Samsung **spawned** media stories that they refused selfies with fans carrying an Apple phone. This resulted in images of concert fans customising their iPhones to resemble a Samsung model. As their international acclaim broadened, the Korean cosmetics they endorse **flew off the shelves**. Band members now model for, among others, Dior, Chanel and Celine.

* sassy: 멋진(=stylish, chic)
* burnish: 빛나게 하다(=polish, shine)
* spawn: 낳다, 일으키다
* fly off the shelves: 날개 돋친 듯 팔리다(=sell very quickly)

"Focus on Terminology"

◈ A-List performers

A-list는 미국 연예계 언론인 James Ulmer가 2011년 전 세계 영화배우 1400명을 수익성 기준으로 분류한 *The Hot List*에서 가장 상위 층 목록을 가리킨다. Ulmer scale이라 불리는 *The Hot List*는 전체 6개의 목록들로 구성되어 있다: A+, A, B+, B, C, 그리고 D. 요즈음에는 영화 산업을 벗어나 'A-list singers' 'A-list celebrities'처럼 다양한 영역에서 사용되고 있다. 재미를 위해서 또는 과장된 표현으로 (대중들에게 전혀 알려지지 않은 사람을 지칭할 때 또는 자기 스스로를 비하할 때) E-list 심지어 Z-list라는 표현을 사용하기도 한다.

Eight years into their career, Grammy-nominated BTS view the US as a secure domain. It achieved five Billboard chart-toppers faster than any band since the Beatles. Almost one million people in 191 countries paid to view two virtual concerts from Seoul last year. In May 2021, their star power was polished by a cameo in the *Friends: The Reunion TV show*.

Having built their brand stature, frequent stylistic reinvention is needed to sustain it. Both bands are famed for their bold fashions, haircuts and postures which identify them as individual idols, as well as fashion collectives.

In the case of BTS, **gender-fluid** eye and lip colorings and a **CGI-like androgyny** attain a rare unisex appeal. This has earned lucrative contracts with skincare and fashion brands. The boys recently starred in Louis Vuitton's **sumptuous** Fall/Winter collection video show filmed at Art Bunker B39 near Seoul.

As a priceless national asset, BTS is also the face of tourism for the Korean capital Seoul, and features in promotions by the Korea Tourism Organisation. Provinces nation-wide create self-guided tours inspired by the beaches and beauty spots captured in BTS videos.

BTS Bus Stop at Jumunjin Beach source: www.habkorea.net

* gender-fluid: 특정한 성별로 인식되지 않는(=not strictly identifying as one distinct gender)
* CGI(computer-generated imagery)-like androgyny: 컴퓨터로 만든 이미지 같은 양성 (兩性)의 특징들
* sumptuous: 화려한

Band Unity vs Individual Temptations
The BTS 'Army' and Blackpink 'Blinks' fans in South East Asia are undeniably youthful. So is their commercial success the outcome of **Gen Z** social media obsessions, TikTok dance challenges and a desire to "shine on stage" like their idols?

Largely, but not wholly
While the brand universe is segmenting between those who can recite the member names of BTS (RM, Jin, Suga, J-Hope, Jimin, V, and Jung Kook) and Blackpink (Jennie, Lisa, Rosé and Jisoo) and those who can't, their appeal is more **cross-cutting** than it may appear.

Beyond social media, BTS and Blackpink are content generation machines. In recent weeks, BTS featured in publications ranging from National Geographic, Reuters and CNN to The Jakarta Post, Hindustan Times, and Travel Weekly Asia. None of those titles explicitly targets a Gen Z readership. Pepsi and McDonald's also enjoy diverse customer bases.

That said, their burgeoning associations with luxury fashion houses is resonating with Gen Z's across Asian—especially China, the region's largest and toughest consumer market.

* cross-cutting: 전통적으로 분리된 집단/관심사를 연결하는

Focus on Terminology

◈ Generation Z (Gen Z)

1990년대 중후반부터 2010년 초반에 태어난 세대를 지칭하는데 zoomers라 부르기도 한다. 대부분 Generation X의 자손들이며, 그들 다음 세대는 Generation Alpha이다.

Five generations. source: www.aberley.com

The international brand success scored by BTS and Blackpink is unprecedented for Asian stars. And while the relentless marketing drives will continue, future pathways are less clear.

Longevity concerns exist, particularly given the challenges that superstardom creates. K-Pop's production line is littered with burned out stars who once shone brightly. Band members are subject to constant social media scrutiny and press intrusion. They must diet strictly, train constantly and **eschew** personal relationships. The emotional strain is intense.

This theme was analysed by Korean American documentary maker Joi Lee, in her new series *Deciphering South Korea*. "K-Pop has given Koreans so much pride in their nation's creativity and musical talent. But I am concerned about how much this industry requires from the people who keep it running," she says.

* eschew: 삼가다(=refrain, abstain), 피하다

◇ 빈 칸에 들어갈 단어를 위 글에서 찾아 문장을 완성해봅시다.

1. When they ____________ order and discipline, they pay a steep price: chaotic operations and unpredictable performance.
2. With the right support, we can all take ____________ in our achievements, whether they are in the classroom or on a playing field.
3. The catastrophe that made all of that a distant memory was equally ____________ in the history of mankind.
4. The campaign is part of a ____________ to make Bradford Shopping Center a safer and more pleasant place to shop.
5. I can't keep my mind focused for hour after hour and my body won't take the ____________ for so long, either.
6. People say that once you walk into public life you have to accept the kind of interest and ____________ that always follows.
7. Here is a young man whose ____________ pursuit of excellence is conducted with single-minded determination.

Plus, the **oft-touted** band unity concept is entering a notoriously tricky phase: solo projects. Individual **enticements** have proved **thorny** for popular bands ranging from the Jackson Five and The Supremes to NSYNC, Destiny's Child, the Spice Girls and One Direction.

Those groups were, of course, **forged** in the western hemisphere. The pressures and rewards are different in today's hyper-networked, brand-centric world.

With the ascension from pop band to global brand **crystallising**, time will tell whether any, or all, of these 11 young Koreans is able to **redraft** the rules of superstardom.

* oft-touted: 화제에 많이 오른, 많이 홍보된(=frequently praised/publicized)
* enticement: 유혹하는 것
* thorny: 곤란한, 가시처럼 날카로운
* forge: 공들여 만들다(=form or make by concentrated effort)
* crystallise: 확고해지다, 명확해지다
* redraft: 고쳐 쓰다(=alter, modify)

band 활동을 하다 solo로 전향한 예

Michael Jackson in the Jackson Five
source: www.reidlee.com

Zayn Malik while in One Direction
source: www.billboard.com

1. 다음의 단어들을 사용하여 빈 칸을 채워봅시다.

attend conferred assignment envoy adopted accompany

The members of K-pop superstar boy band BTS—already the face of South Korean soft power on the world stage, have now taken on a formal diplomatic role as "special presidential _________ for future generations and culture." In a ceremony in Seoul on Tuesday, South Korean President Moon Jae-in _________ the title upon the newly minted celebrity diplomats, handing them diplomatic passports and their first _________: To _________ him to the 76th session of the United Nations General Assembly in New York, which opened Tuesday. The group is set to _________ a meeting on the U.N. Sustainable Development Goals, _________ by all U.N. member states in 2015.

2. 괄호 안 단어를 활용하여 적절한 표현으로 빈 칸을 채워봅시다.

a. Although K-pop generally refers to South Korean pop music, some consider it to be an all-encompassing genre ____________ (exhibit) a wide spectrum of musical and visual elements.

b. When combining multiple singers, the singers often switch their positions while singing and dancing by making prompt movements in synchrony, a strategy ____________ (call) "formation changing".

c. While male idol groups' costumes were constructed with similar color schemes, fabrics, and styles, the outfits worn by each member still maintained ____________ (individual).

d. K-pop management companies have been criticized for ____________ (exploit) of idols through overwork and restrictive contracts, described as "slave contracts".

e. In an age of mass communication, soft power ____________ (regard) as a more effective and pragmatic diplomatic tactic than the traditional diplomatic strategy hard power.

BTS McDonald's Meal Sparks Frenzy and Store Closures in Indonesia

K-pop group BTS' limited-edition branded McDonald's meals were so hot in Indonesia this week that dozens of stores had to close for fear that the crowds **clamoring** for them would spread COVID-19. The meal debuted locally on Wednesday, and demand quickly overwhelmed stores. Most Indonesian customers had placed their orders online due to the pandemic, leading to huge crowds of motorcycle-taxi deliverymen left queuing for hours inside and outside stores—and raising concerns that the circumstances could lead to a super-spreader event.

source: www.bbc.com

Jakarta police have ordered 32 McDonald's stores to temporarily close for "violating health **protocols**" by failing to limit capacity to 50% and enforce social-distancing measures. A police spokesman told the local press that authorities have even asked that the BTS meal be temporarily put on hold altogether.

* frenzy: 광란(=hysteria, craze)
* clamor: 떠들썩하게 요구하다(=make insistent demands)
* protocol: 행동 규칙(=code of correct conduct)

◇ 다음 단어와 반대의 의미를 지닌 단어를 위 글에서 찾아봅시다.

1. permit (v.)	2. broadly	3. permanently
4. comply	5. partly	6. calmness

Other cities have had to close McDonald's stores as well. Fajar Purwoto, the public order agency head for the central Javan port city of Semarang, explained to AFP that the **municipality** had temporarily shuttered four of its six McDonald's for a few days. "I don't want Semarang to be in the COVID-19 red zone again," he said.
Indonesia is one of the Asian countries hardest hit by the virus. New daily cases have gone up 26% in the last two weeks, and only 4% of Indonesians are fully vaccinated, according to data from the New York Times.
The coveted BTS meal includes nuggets, fries, a drink and limited-edition sweet chili and cajun sauces in purple packaging **emblazoned** with the band's logo. Anticipating that a purchasing frenzy would occur once the meals became available, Indonesian fans encouraged each other to tip drivers well and donate funds to give back to those **braving** potential COVID-19 exposure to bring them their nuggets. One fund-raising campaign run by the group BTS ARMY Indonesia has raised over $18,000 so far. ARMY is a global term used to refer to the band's fans.

* municipality: 시(市) 당국
* emblazon: 새기다, 장식하다(=inscribe)
* brave: 용감히 맞서다(=face courageously)

BTS meal packaging on sale. source: www.ebay.com

"It's great when we can share our happiness with others. This time, let's share it with the [delivery] drivers," its main page said in Indonesian. "They will be our heroes ordering the BTS meal, dedicating their time to waiting and delivering the special food directly to each ARMY's home. By sharing, this BTS anniversary and BTS meal celebration will not just make us happy, but also make our fan activities a blessing!"
The meal will release in almost 50 other countries. It first hit Asia in Malaysia late last month. As COVID-19 numbers rise across the region, other Asian countries have grown concerned that the meal's popularity could spark **pandemonium** and crowds. Singapore actually delayed the meal's debut by a month to help people comply with a new round of stricter distancing rules.
Now, the Philippines is preparing to **batten down the hatches**. McDonald's there issued a statement ahead of the meal's local release stating that it's preparing to enforce COVID-19 safety measures and to meet the huge demand, according to local news reports.

* pandemonium: 대혼란(=chaos)

"Focus on Vocabulary"

◆ batten down the hatches

'위기에 대비하다(get ready for difficult times)'를 뜻하는데, 배가 항해할 때 몰려오는 폭풍우에 대비하여 갑판(deck)의 승강구(hatch)를 큰 나무 널빤지(batten)로 덮는데서 (화살표 가리키는 곳) 유래한 표현이다.

source: https://adventuresofkate.co.uk

BTS Meal 시식 후기

"I want to be a nugget. I want to be a chili sauce."

"The sweet chili and Cajun sauces have never been available in the US before, so I was stoked to try them out for the first time. However, the sweet chili was just a spicier version of the sweet and sour sauce, and the Cajun sauce basically tastes like barbecue and mayo mixed together."

＊ stoke: 감정을 돋우다(=stir up)

"Sweet chili was my fav tbh, I thought it would be more special tho? Kinda ... disappointed☹"

＊ fav: favorite, tbh: to be honest, tho: though

"The centerpiece of the BTS Meal is that the boys actually introduced two new menu items: Cajun and Sweet Chili dipping sauces. You already know what McNuggets taste like (little beige clouds sent down from heaven itself). You already know about fries and Coke. But these sauces are gorgeous. They are the new eighth and ninth members of BTS. The attractive packaging in shades of millennial pink and lilac fits BTS's current aesthetic perfectly, with Korean lettering on the labels to make this one of the more authentic experiences you can have in a McDonald's."

"BTS is a great band, but it always kills me when fast food restaurants make a "new meal" when really it's nothing new, they just add one small thing. People will pay extra just for the name."

"I went every single day to get the BTS Meal since launch to get the bag. I now have the bag!! It is the first BTS merch I have ever been able to get. I am so happy. Sweet chili was my fav. I loathed Cajun, but that it is because I don't like horseradish."

＊ merch: merchandise, horseradish: 서양고추냉이

"just tried it and its so tasty and yummy! 10/10! and I love the limited edition bag!"

"Me eating the BTS meal 24/7 and then starting crying for no reason"

< Popular Internet/Chat Slang >

2day: Today
2moro: Tomorrow
2nite: Tonight
4AO: For Adults Only
4EAE: For Ever And Ever
AAMOF: As A Matter Of Fact
ABT: About
ADIH: Another Day In Hell
ADN: Any Day Now
AFAIC: As Far As I'm Concerned
AFAICT: As Far As I Can Tell
AFAIK: As Far As I Know
AFAIR: As Far As I Remember
AFK: Away From Keyboard
AKA: Also Known As
AMA: Ask Me Anything
ASAIC: As Soon As I Can
ASAP: As Soon As Possible
ATM: At The Moment
AYMM: Are You My Mother?
AYOR: At Your Own Risk
B@U: Back At You
B4: Before
B4N: Bye For Now
BAE: Before Anyone Else
BBBG: Bye Bye Be Good
BBIAS: Be Back In A Sec
BBL: Be Back Later
BBT: Be Back Tomorrow
BCNU: Be Seeing You
BD: Big Deal
BFF: Best Friends Forever
BMT: Before My Time
BOL: Be On Later
BOT: Back On Topic
BRB: Be Right Back
BRO: Brother
BSAAW: Big Smile And A Wink
BT: But
BTW: By The Way
BUMP: Bring Up My Post
BWL: Bursting With Laughter
CFY: Calling For You
CSL: Can't Stop Laughing
CU: See You
CUL: See You Later
Cuz: Because
CWOT: Complete Waste Of Time
CYT: See You Tomorrow
DAE: Does Anyone Else?
DBMIB: Don't Bother Me I'm Busy
DFTBA: Don't Forget To Be Awesome!
DIKU: Do I Know You?
DIY: Do It Yourself
DM: Direct Message
DND: Do Not Disturb
DR: Double Rainbow
DWBH: Don't Worry, Be Happy
DWH: During Work Hours
E123: Easy As One, Two, Three
ELI5: Explain Like I'm 5
EMBM: Early Morning Business Meeting
EOM: End Of Message
EOS: End Of Story
F2F: Face To Face
FAQ: Frequently Asked Question
FAWC: For Anyone Who Cares
FB: Facebook
FBF: Flash Back Friday
FF: Final Fantasy
FIFY: Fixed It For You
FIMH: Forever In My Heart
FITB: Fill In The Blank
FOMO: Fear Of Missing Out
FTFY: Fixed That For You
FTL: For The Loss[1]
FTW: For The Win
FWB: Friends With Benefits
FWIW: For What It's Worth
FYE: For Your Entertainment
FYEO: For Your Eyes Only
FYI: For Your Information
G2G: Got To Go
GA: Go Ahead

GAHOY: Get A Hold of Yourself
GAL: Get A Life
GFN: Gone For Now
GL: Good Luck
GM: Good Morning
GMTA: Great Minds Think Alike
GN: Good Night
GOI: Get Over It
Gr8: Great
GRAS: Generally Recognised As Safe
GRATZ: Congratulations
GTR: Getting Ready
HAND: Have A Nice Day
HB: Hurry Back
HBD: Happy Birthday
HBU: How About You
HMB: Hit Me Back
HMU: Hit Me Up[2]
HRU: How Are You
HTH: Hope This Helps
IAC: In Any Case
IANAL: I Am Not A Lawyer
IC: I See
ICYMI: In Case You Missed It
IDC: I Don't Care
IDK: I Don't Know
IFYP: I Feel Your Pain
IG: Instagram
IIRC: If I Remember Correctly
IKR: I Know Right
ILY: I Love You
IMHO: In My Humble Opinion
IMMD: It Made My Day
IMO: In My Opinion
IMU: I Miss You
IMY: I Miss You
IRL: In Real Life
IS: I'm Sorry
ISO: In Search Of
IU2U: It's Up To You
J4F: Just For Fun
JAM: Just A Minute
JFY: Just For You
JIC: Just In Case
JK: Just Kidding
JSYK: Just So You Know
KK: Okay
L8: Late
L8R: Later
LMA: Leave Me Alone
LMAO: Laughing My A** Off
LMBO: Laughing My Butt Off
LMK: Let Me Know
LOL: Laughing Out Loud
LTNS: Long Time No See
LYLAS: Love You Like A Sister
M/F: Male or Female
M8: Mate
MFW: My Face When[3]
MP: My Pleasure
MRW: My Reaction When
MSG: Message
MSM: Mainstream Media
MU: Miss You
MYOB: Mind Your Own Business
NAGI: Not A Good Idea
NBD: No Big Deal
NE1: Anyone
NFS: Not For Sale
NM: Not Much
NP: No Problem
NSFL: Not Safe For Life[4]
NSFW: Not Safe For Work
NTH: Nice to have
NTS: Note To Self
NVM: Never Mind
OC: Original Content
OFC: Of Course
OH: Overheard
OIC: Oh! I See
OMD: Oh My Damn
OMDB: Over My Dead Body
OMG: Oh My Goodness
OMW: On My Way
OP: Original Poster
OT: Off Topic
PAW: Parents Are Watching
Pls: Please
POTD: Photo Of The Day
POV: Point Of View
PPL: People
PRT: Please Retweet

PTB: Please Text Back
Q4U: Question For You
QQ: Crying
RBTL: Read Between The Lines
RIP: Rest In Peace
RL: Real Life
RLRT: Real Life Retweet
ROFL: Rolling On the Floor Laughing
RT: Retweet
RTM: Read The Manual
RUOK: Are You OK?
SFW: Safe For Work
SIS: Sister
SITD: Still In The Dark
SM: Social Media
SMH: Shaking My Head
SMY: Still Miss You
SNH: Sarcasm Noted Here
SOL: Sooner Or Later
Some1: Someone
SOML: Story Of My Life
SRSLY: Seriously
Str8: Straight
SYS: See You Soon
TBA: To Be Announced
TBH: To Be Honest
TBT: Truth Be Told
TFH: Thread From Hell[5]
TFTI: Thanks For The Invite
TFW That Feeling When
THX: Thanks
TIA: Thanks in Advance
TIL: Today I Learned
TIME: Tears In My Eyes
TINLA: This Is not Legal Advice
TL;DR: Too Long; Didn't Read
TLC: Tender Loving Care
TMB: Tweet Me Back
TMI: Too Much Information
TNTL: Trying Not To Laugh
TTYL: Talk To You Later
TTYS: Talk To You Soon
Txt: Text
TYVM: Thank You Very Much
U4F: You Forever
UR: Your
VBG: Very Big Grin
VSF: Very Sad Face
W8: Wait
WB: Welcome Back
WBU: What About You?
WEG: Wicked Evil Grin
WKND: Weekend
WOM: Word of Mouth
WOTD: Word Of The Day
Wru: Who Are You
WTF: What The F***
WTPA: Where The Party At?
WU?: What's up?
WUZUP: What's up?
WYCM: Will You Call Me?
WYWH: Wish You Were Here
XOXO: Hugs And Kisses
YGM: You've Got Mail
YGTR: You Got That Right
YNK: You Never Know
YOLO: You Only Live Once
YT: YouTube
YW: You're Welcome
ZZZ: Sleeping, Bored, Tired

1. FTL (For The Loss) — 어떤 것의 quality가 낮을 때 사용
2. HMU (Hit Me Up) — "연락해"
3. MFW (My Face When) — 어떤 이미지에 caption으로 넣어 자신의 얼굴 모습이 그 이미지와 같음을 표현할 때 사용
4. NSFL (Not Safe For Life) — 정신적 피해를 줄 수 있을 정도로 충격적/불쾌한/잔인한 content를 지칭할 때 사용
5. TFH (Thread From Hell) — 멈추지 않는 토론을 지칭할 때 사용

Blackpink: What You Need to Know About K-pop's Biggest Girl Group

The four-member South Korean girl band — who get their name from the mixture of tough "black" and **flirty** "pink" of their songs — have been global superstars since the release of their June 2016 single "Boombayah."

Why are they called Blackpink?

Formed by YG Entertainment under the famous K-pop trainee system in South Korea, the members auditioned with the entertainment agency to become students or 'trainees' with the hope of one day making their debut as a recording artist. When Blackpink debuted, their label YG Entertainment said the name intends to convey that the group embodies more than beauty — there's a toughness, too.

"The meaning of BLACKPINK aims to contradict the common perception of the color pink," the statement read. "Pink is commonly used to portray prettiness, but BLACKPINK actually means to say that 'Pretty isn't everything.' It also symbolizes that they are a team that encompasses not only beauty, but also great talent."

BLACKPINK on Spotify	
Songs	Spotify Streams in 2020
Kill This Love	48,893,258
Kiss and Make Up	32,694,455
DDU-DU DDU-DU	26,488,048
Don't Know What To Do	23,082,377
As If It's Your Last	18,693,914
Boombayah	16,723,780
Forever Young	11,967,262
Playing With Fire	11,895,633
Whistle	10,868,888
Kick It	7,332,761
Stay	6,508,046
Really	5,988,889
See U Later	4,911,427
Hope Not	4,544,579
	as of April 30, 2020

source: www.wangzee.com

* flirty: 관능적인, 경박한, 심각하지 않은(=not serious with someone/something)

How is Blackpink different from other K-pop groups?

Between their debut in 2016 and the 2020 release of *The Album*, Blackpink released fewer than 22 songs, all singles. Despite the small **discography**, the group's glam look and fun choreography were quickly replicated by other K-pop groups and fans in their social media videos.

The biggest part of Blackpink's popularity lies in their songs, which talk about independence and vulnerability, bilingual lyrics, and undeniable stage presence. Blackpink is also known for the styling of their videos, otherwise referred to as 'concepts' for each song. Where some K-pop videos might have two or three concepts in their music videos, Blackpink will often have five or six completely different concepts (complete with different hair colors and clothing) featured in their video.

How long has Blackpink been together?

Blackpink debuted in 2016 with the mini album *Square One*, which consisted of only two songs — "Whistle" and "Boombayah." The debut was heavily promoted in the K-pop scene as Blackpink was the first girl group from YG Entertainment in seven years. "Boombayah" **galloped straight out of the gate** to hit No. 1 on Billboard's World Digital Songs chart, and their popularity continued with additional releases in the following year.

* gallop straight out of the gate: (경주마가) 출발하자마자 전속력으로 질주하다

“Focus on Terminology”

◈ discography

특정 artist나 작곡가의 작품을 녹음한 전체 목록 또는 음반을 연구하고 분류하는 것을 지칭하는 용어로 위 문맥에서는 첫 번째 뜻으로 사용하고 있다. disc와 기록(writing)을 뜻하는 graphy가 합쳐진 단어로 1930년대 jazz 레코드 수집가들 사이에서 출처가 뚜렷하지 않은 음악들을 연구하면서 대중적으로 사용되었다.

-graphy는 다양한 분야에서 사용되는데, 영화에서 배우의 출연 목록을 filmography라고 하며, 영화 촬영을 기록으로 남기는 것을 cinematography라고 한다. 그 외 예술 분야에서 calligraphy(서예), choreography(안무) 등의 표현이 있다.

In 2018, Blackpink made headlines again with their single "Ddu-Du Ddu-Du" from the **EP** *Square Up*. A few months later, the group branched out by working with Dua Lipa on the track "Kiss and Make Up."
YG Entertainment positioned Blackpink for a global market by partnering with Interscope Records and Universal Music Group in October 2018. **In short order**, Blackpink then focused on the U.S. market with performances on *The Late Show with Stephen Colbert*, *Good Morning America*, and the 2019 Coachella music festival.

What about Blackpink songs?
For an introduction to Blackpink music, start with them at the beginning: their debut single "Boombayah." The video for the song has an upbeat and fun girls-night-out vibe (ending in a party at a retro rollerskating rink). The video offers viewers a peek at the group's impending stardom with sharp choreography and a **flair** for visuals.
Next, move on to "Ddu-Du Ddu-Du"—the 2018 comeback single is a rapid-fire **whirlwind** of tough-girl cool; follow up with "Whistle," "As If It's Your Last," "Lovesick Girls," and "Playing With Fire," each of which have introspective melodies with lyrics full of love, eagerness, and passion. The track "Ice Cream," on the other hand, is a rare sexy song from the group, showcasing **double entendre** lyrics against a hypnotic beat. Check out the animated version of the video to see Blackpink rendered as Zepeto—an app that allows users to turn themselves into 3D animated characters.

* EP: Extended Play. mini album의 확장판
* in short order: 곧장(=quickly, with no delay)
* flair: 재능, 능력, 기술
* whirlwind: 회오리바람, 정신없이 달려드는 것

Focus on Terminology

◈ double entendre

'이중적 의미'를 지닌 표현을(위 글에서 Ice Cream/I scream) 지칭한다. 해당하는 표현의 한 가지 의미는 뚜렷한 반면, 다른 의미는 '사회적으로 불편한 이슈에 대한,' '반정부 성향의,' 또는 '성적으로 암시하는' 의미를 내포한다. Triple entendre는 '세 가지 의미'를 지닌 표현을 지칭.

"Pretty Savage" and "Crazy Over You," songs from the band's new album, highlights the group's vocal **prowess**, with maple syrup smooth lyrics against a **can't-get-it-out-of-your-head** melody. "Bet You Wanna" featuring Cardi B, is a fun song for the band, with bubblegum pop lyrics meant for summertime pool parties or dancing in the kitchen while you make dinner.
End with fan favorites "Kill This Love" and "How You Like That" to see how the group has grown into its own: the two songs showcase girl power, **sick** beats, and **in-your-face** optimism.

What does 'Blackpink in your area' mean?
The band's signature phrase, first uttered in their debut song "Boombayah," declares the group's global domination plan. With every new song, Blackpink teases **snippets** of new concepts, hair colors, and clothing. And boy, the publicity has paid off. The group now has over 54 million subscribers on their YouTube channel—with the video for "Kill This Love" currently sitting at over 1.1 billion views.

source: www.blackpinkyg.com

* prowess: 뛰어난 스킬, 능력
* can't-get-it-out-of-your-head: 잊을 수 없는
* sick: (slang으로) outstanding
* in-your-face: 대담한(=bold), 공격적인
* snippet: 작은 조각, 소량(=a small piece/bit)

Loyal fans count everything from each member's line distribution on songs to who keeps the center position in the choreography. Blackpink, eager to give the fans what they want, often upload practice videos of the group practicing their choreography. The practice video for "*Lovesick Girls*" has 96 million views at the time of this writing.
Fans also **flock** to what's known as 'fancams'—concert videos that focus on one member of the group's performance. Search for 'Blackpink fancam' on YouTube, and you'll find dozens of videos from each of their live performances, each highlighting one member at a time. The popularity of Blackpink means new business ventures for its members: Jisoo has signed as a Dior ambassador, Jennie for Chanel, Rosé for Saint Laurent, and Lisa for Celine.
Netflix paired with Blackpink to air their documentary *Light Up The Sky*—a first look behind the scenes of the inner workings of the band. For a peek into the (almost) off-duty personality of the band, look for 'Blackpink 24/365' on YouTube. The program, the title of which is a reference to a line from their song "Whistle," is set in a Big Brother-type camera-outfitted house, is a hub where the bandmates live during the promotional periods surrounding new singles.

* flock: 몰려들다

< Top Seven Most Viewed Fancams on Youtube in 2020 >

	Singer	Song	Views
1	BTS V	On	21.5 million
2	BTS Jungkook	On	13.6 million
3	Blackpink Rosé	Someone You Loved	12.1 million
4	Ailee	Stand Up For Love	11.3 million
5	BTS Jimin	On	11.1 million
6	ITZY Ryunjin	Wannabe	9.2 million
7	BTS V	Black Swan	7.5 million

source: www.patreon.com

'How You Like That' official music video에 대한 댓글 모음

♪ If BLACKPINK will attend MAMA, it will be a bomb.

* MAMA: Mnet Asian Music Awards

♪ Who wants this bop to hit 1 billion soon?

* bop: 춤추기에 좋은 음악. bebop의 줄임말.

♪ This song is a banger! I like how the song started soft. The build up is so good. I got chills all over my body, really! And when the drop came, I'm like.... uhm yeah! I really really like this. Can't stop myself from repeating it. Ughhhh, this is so good. 1, 2, 3 Ha How you like that?

* banger: 대단한 노래. drop: 사운드가 떨어졌다 올라가는 부분

♪ If u think that they deserve AOTY, SOTY, and all the FEMALE CATEGORY ..... then don't just think and sit ...... str3am and vot3 .... str3am blinks str3am...... before its too late .....

* AOTY: Album of the Year, SOTY: Song of the Year, str3am: stream, vot3: vote

♪ Guys, the number of views is not important. The main thing is that we must be happy that our queens finally hit us with that comeback. And also if they are comfortable with it :)

♪ I think the reason yg rarely makes blackpink comeback is because it's big. And when I say big, it's just BIG. Like just look at those background props damn. Their mvs are so grand it's like throwing money everywhere. I'm not complaining tho

♪ I wish jisoo said "Black pink in your area" the beginning of the song.

♪ I feel like the beat and the lyrics are appealing to both men and women—not all songs are like that.

♪ Blinks don't hate ARMY and ARMY don't hate Blinks!! These are just haters of both groups!!!

* hater: 악플을 다는 사람

♪ Lisa and Jennie : Look at you now look at me
Me: quickly grab a mirror

♪ My 4 year old son loves this song so much. He calls this song "the scary one" LOL.

♪ They've never disappointed us. But YG on the other hand..... yeah they suck

♪ OMG THE BEAT IN LISA'S RAP SOUNDS LIKE ALADDIN

1. 다음의 단어들을 사용하여 빈 칸을 채워봅시다.

complete staged tied stunned attended accessorize respectively

Latest BLACKPINK member to make an appearance at Paris Fashion Week, Jennie conquered the front row of Chanel's Spring/Summer 2022 show today in one of her chicest outfits yet.

Following her bandmates Jisoo and Rosé, who __________ the Dior and Saint Laurent show __________ last week, Jennie became the star attraction in Paris as soon as she arrived at the Place Joffre, where Chanel's very nostalgic SS22 runway was __________. The K-pop singer, who has been a house ambassador for Chanel since 2018, __________ in a coral red bouclé tweed set comprised of a cropped vest and a mini skirt. To __________, she layered a pearl choker with a double "C" logo necklace, stacked up the Coco Crush rings, and wore a glass pearl belt around the waist. Of course, the look wouldn't be __________ without a quilted leather handbag from Chanel—Jennie's bag of choice comes in bright red and features golden hardware. A chic pair of sandal heels adorned with black bows __________ everything together.

Just before today's presentation, Jennie was also spotted in a series of promotional videos for the new collection, in which she poses alongside other ambassadors and friends of Chanel like Lily-Rose Depp and Quannah Chasinghorse.

2. 괄호 안 단어를 활용하여 적절한 표현으로 빈 칸을 채워봅시다.

a. As an ambassador for the legendary French house, Jennie showed up looking ____________ (flame) hot in a vibrant crimson red Chanel set.

b. Rosé attended Saint Laurent's spring 2022 show on Sept. 28, whose runway was overlooking a brightly ____________ (light) Eiffel Tower.

c. Jisoo stunned us all in a white wool and silk mini dress from Dior's Cruise 2022 collection, ____________ (pair) with a micro Lady Dior bag that she was one of the first to show off.

SM Entertainment to launch US-based K-pop group through new TV series

SM Entertainment has partnered with production company MGM Worldwide Television Group for a new K-pop competition TV series. According to a report by *The Hollywood Reporter*, the companies have linked up to develop a show that look for young talents to form a brand-new US-based K-pop boyband. The show will scout for "America's most talented emerging artists" and feature participants between the ages of 13 to 25.

The new K-pop group, called NCT-Hollywood, will be the newest addition to the currently 23-member supergroup NCT. The supergroup is comprised of several sub-units, including the Seoul-based NCT 127, the China-based WayV, a fixed seven-member group NCT Dream and rotational unit NCT U.

Successful contestants will fly to Seoul, South Korea to attend "K-pop **bootcamp**" at SM Entertainment. In each episode, contestants will compete in dance, vocal and style tests where they will be judged and mentored by SM founder Lee Soo-Man and NCT members.

Metro Goldwyn Mayer TELEVISION

Mark Burnett, Chairman of MGM Television. source: www.logopedia.com

* bootcamp: 집중 훈련 프로그램(intensive training program), 군대의 신병 훈련소

"I look forward to making an **unconventional** audition show that all music fans around the world can enjoy," Lee said in a statement. "I hope the audience enjoys watching the journey of new stars being born in Hollywood, that will be promoted as NCT-Hollywood in the global market in the future."

"This series is exactly the type of innovative programming that MGM is committed to creating on a global scale," added MGM Television chairman Mark Burnett. "K-pop is more than a genre of music; it's a cultural phenomenon and we're so excited to partner with the incredible Soo-Man Lee and the team at SM to bring K-pop to the U.S."

SM Entertainment's upcoming TV competition is the second such reality series to be announced in recent days. Earlier this week, HBO Max and CJ ENM revealed that they were currently in the development stages of an as-yet-untitled K-pop talent series based in Latin America.

* unconventional: 색다른, 독창적인(=original)

Focus on Terminology

◆ singing audition 관련 용어

8-bars, 16-bars, 32-bars	audition에서 통상적으로 제한하는 노래의 길이로 8, 16, 32 마디를 의미. 대략적으로 각각 30초, 1분, 2분 이내의 시간.
a cappella	반주 없이 목소리로만 노래 부르기
catch breath	노래 가사 중간에 하는 빠른 호흡
diction	단어들을 뚜렷하게 발음하기
call back	2차 audition이나 인터뷰에 초대
intonation	음높이를 뜻하는데, 원하는 음보다 한 음 낮게 부르거나(sing flat) 높게 부르는(sing sharp) 경우 bad intonation을 가지고 있다고 함.
repertoire	가수가 잘 알고, 잘 부를 수 있는 노래 모음
resonance	들숨의 공기를 허파에 저장했다가 허파로부터 날숨의 공기를 성대로 통과시킬 때 진동시켜 만드는 소리로 공명(共鳴)이라 부름.
sight reading	연습 없이 현장에서 악보 읽기

< Acronyms and Full Names of Major Entertainment Sources >

Acronym	Full Name	Acronym	Full Name
A&M	Alpert's and Moss's	I Records	Interscope Records
AMG	Access Media Group	LBW	Lil' Bow Wow
BMG	Bertelsmann Music Group	MCU	Marvel Cinematic Universe
CAA	Creative Artists Agency	MGM	Metro-Goldwyn Mayer
CHTR	Charter Communications Inc.	NCS	NoCopyrightSounds
CMCSA	Comcast Corp.	OVO	October's Very Own
DIS	The Walt Disney Co.	QC	Quality Control Music
ECM	Edition of Contemporary Music	RCA	Radio Corporation of America
EMI	Electric and Musical Industries	SME	Sony Music Entertainment
ESPN	Entertainment and Sports Programming Network	TBS	Turner Broadcasting System
		UA	United Artists
FH	Fame House	UME	Universal Music Enterprises
FNC	Fish and Cake	UMG	Universal Music Group
FXM	FX Movie Channel	UTA	United Talent Agency
GOOD	Getting Out Our Dreams	VEVO	Video Evolution
G-Unit	Guerilla Unit Records	VH1	Video Hits One
HBO	Home Box Office	Viacom	Video & Audio Communications
HMV	His Master's Voice	WB	Warner Brothers
ICM	International Creative Management	WME	William Morris Endeavor
ILG	Independent Label Group	WMG	Warner Music Group

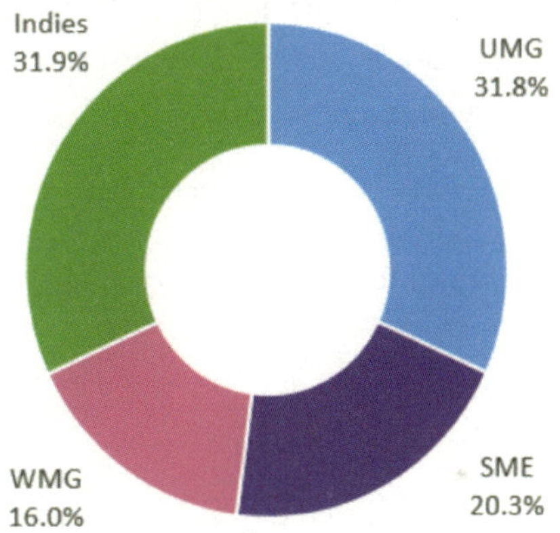

Global label market share (2019)
source: www.digitalmusicnews.com

Former Big Bang Member Seungri Gets Three Year Prison Term in Prostitution Case

A South Korean military court **sentenced** disgraced K-pop star Seungri to three years in prison on Thursday (August 12) for crimes including providing prostitutes to foreign businessmen. The Defense Ministry said the former member of the boy band Big Bang was also fined 1.15 billion won ($989,000). He was taken into **custody** after the ruling by an army court in Yongin, near Seoul.

Seungri, whose real name is Lee Seung-hyun, was **indicted** in January 2020 on multiple **charges**, including arranging illegal sexual services for business investors from Taiwan, Japan and Hong Kong from 2015 to 2016. He was also **convicted** of **embezzling** funds from a Seoul nightclub he ran and violating laws prohibiting overseas gambling by betting heavily at foreign casinos from 2013 to 2017. He denied most of the charges.

His case was transferred to a military court after he **enlisted** in the army in March last year for 21 months of military service, a requirement for most able-bodied men in South Korea because of the threat from rival North Korea. Yonhap news agency reported that Seungri appeared in court in a combat uniform and shook his head repeatedly as the judge announced the **verdict**. Before his fall from grace, Seungri was one of the biggest stars in K-pop because of the success of Big Bang, which attracted huge followings in Asia and other parts of the world after its debut in 2006.

Forbes magazine reported in 2016 that the group had made $44 million in pretax earnings the previous year. Seungri left the group in 2019 after the media reported the prostitution **accusations**. His case is one of several scandals that have roiled South Korea's entertainment industry in recent years.

* enlist: 입대하다(=enter the armed forces)

Focus on Terminology

◈ Seungri 관련 기사에서 사용된 legal terms

sentence (v.)	형을 선고하다. sentence somebody to + 형벌
custody (n.)	구속(=confinement). warrant of custody = 구속영장
indict (v.)	기소하다. suspension of indictment = 기소 유예
charge (n.)	혐의. bring a charge = 고발하다
convict (v.)	유죄 판결을 내리다. 명사 뜻은 기결수, 죄수
embezzle (v.)	횡령하다. embezzlement (n.)
verdict (n)	판결. verdict of acquittal = 무죄 판결
accusation	고소. false accusation = 무고

◈ Other essential legal terms

가석방	parole	소환장	writ of summons
검사	prosecutor	심신미약	mental weakness
경범죄	minor offense / misdemeanor	압수수색영장	warrant of search and confiscation / seizure
과실	negligence	원고	plaintiff
금고	imprisonment without labor	유언	will
기각하다	dismiss	중범죄	felony
맞고소	counterclaim	중재	arbitration
명예훼손	defamation / slander / libel	증거인멸	destruction of evidence
미필적 고의	willful negligence	증언	testimony
민사소송	civil procedure	진술서	written statement
배심원	jury	집행유예	probation
보석(금)	bail	체포영장	warrant of arrest
불기소처분	non-prosecution disposition	피고(인)	defendant
사기	fraud / deceit	피의자	suspect
상고	appeal	합의금	settlement money
상급심	superior / higher court	현행범	flagrant offender
소멸	termination / extinguishment	형사소송	criminal procedure

참고: 법령용어 한영사전. 법제처

승리 사건의 판결에 대한 해외 media headlines

- Seungri: Former K-pop star jailed for gambling and organising sex work — BBC
- Seungri prostitution case: K-pop star fined 1.15 billion and sentenced to 3 years in jail; fans stand by singer while netizen demand harsher punishment — The Times of India
- K-Pop Idol Seungri Jailed For 3 Years Along With A Fine Of 1.15 Billion For Prostitution And Fraud Scandal — The ED Times
- Disgraced K-pop star Seungri sentenced to three years on prostitution charges — CNN
- Disgraced K-pop star Seungri jailed for prostitution, gambling ring — www.pagesix.com
- K-Pop Icon Seungri Gets Prison for Pimping Prostitutes, Gambling With Millions — VegasSlotsOnline
- Ex K-pop star Seungri jailed for 3 years for arranging prostitution: reports Seoul — The Independent Singapore News
- Former BigBang Member Seungri Sentenced to Three Years in Prison on Sex Scandal Charges Along with a ₩1.15 billion KRW ($990,000 USD) fine — Hyperbeast
- VERDICT | Former BigBang Seungri receives 3-year sentence in prison — Business Mirror
- K-Pop Star Seungri Sentenced to 3 Years in Prison Following Conviction in Prostitution Case — www.people.com
- Ex-BigBang Member Seungri Sentenced To 3 Years In Prison For Arranging Sex Services — World of Buzz
- Prostitution Scandal Lands K-Pop Star Seungri in Prison for Three Years — The Daily Beast
- Disgraced K-pop star Seungri could face 5-year jail term from sex, gambling scandal — The Star
- K-pop star Seungri gets 3 years in prison for prostitution, gambling scandal — The NY Daily News

Cross-word Puzzle

ACROSS

2. to strive to equal by imitation
5. a code of correct conduct
6. a natural talent
8. highly attractive
10. quick and skillful
11. brilliant, showy splendor
12. a small piece of anything
15. causing difficulty or distress

DOWN

1. a dreamy romantic quality or feeling
3. to produce in large number
4. not fanciful
7. greatly desired
8. to make shiny or smooth
9. to move rapidly
13. to keep away from
14. a state of wild excitement

Chapter III

K-MOVIE

Parasite makes Oscars history as first foreign language winner of best picture

After an awards season marked by its predictability, the Oscars delivered a spectacular **final-reel twist** on Sunday evening, naming **capitalist satire** 'Parasite' best picture.

source: www.abc.com

Bong Joon-ho's comedy-drama about an impoverished family who **infiltrate** the household of a wealthier one is the first film not in the English language to take the top prize. It also took best director, best **original screenplay** and best international film.

Sam Mendes's *1917* had been **tipped** to rule triumphant at this year's Academy Awards, following its key victories at the **Baftas**, Golden Globes and crucial **bellwethers** such as the Producers **Guild** Awards. In the event, the **harrowing** first world war drama took three awards: for Roger Deakins' **cinematography** and for its visual effects and sound mixing.

* final-reel twist: final-reel은 영화 촬영 필름의 마지막 부분으로 영화의 마지막 장면을 의미한다. final-reel twist는 마지막 순간의 (극적) 반전을 뜻함.
* capitalist satire: 자본주의 풍자
* infiltrate: 잠입하다(=move into a place/organization with hostile intent)
* original screenplay: 각본 cf. adapted screenplay 각색
* tip: 예상하다
* Baftas: British Academy of Film and Television Arts
* bellwether: 전조(a person or thing that indicates a trend), 목에 방울을 걸고 무리를 이끄는 양
* guild: (관심이나 목적이 같은 사람들의) 조합(an organization of people with same interests or goals)
* harrowing: 잔혹한, 끔직한(=extremely painful)
* cinematography: 촬영

source: www.nytimes.com

Bong's film also defeated *Once Upon a Time in Hollywood*, *Jojo Rabbit* and *The Irishman* to best picture. It marks the first time in 65 years—since *Marty* in 1955—that the winner of the **Palme d'Or** at Cannes has progressed to a best picture Oscar.

Bong paid tribute to **Scorsese** in his best director speech, saying that, when he was young, he "carved deep into my heart" a quote by Scorsese: "The most personal is the most creative."

* Palme d'Or (황금 야자수: golden palm) at Cannes: the highest prize awarded at the Cannes Film Festival. Previously, the highest prize at the festival was the Grand Prix du Festival International du Film.
* Martin Charles Scorsese: 이탈리아 태생 미국 영화감독. *The Irishman*의 제작자 겸 감독

기생충 촬영지. 서울시 아현동. 사진: 김경석.

< Parasite 수상 관련 media headlines >

'Parasite' makes Oscars history as the first foreign-language film to win best picture — The Washington Post

Oscars 2020: South Korea's 'Parasite' makes history by winning best picture — BBC

'Parasite' Oscar win is 'a remarkable chapter in Korean culture' — CNN

South Koreans explode with joy over 'Parasite' Oscar wins — AP News

Breaking the subtitle barrier: South Koreans celebrate historic Oscar wins of 'Parasite' — Reuters

'Parasite' wins best picture in least-watched oscars ever — Bloomberg

Trump scoffs at 'Parasite' for Oscars win — NBC

< Critic Reviews >

In Bong Joon Ho's new film, a **destitute** family occupies a wealthy household in an elaborate scheme that goes comically—then horribly—wrong. — The New York Times

With an insightful and **searing** exploration of human behavior, 'Parasite' is a masterfully crafted film that is a definite must watch. — The Times of India

Thrilling and devastating, 'Parasite' is one of the year's very best movies. — The Los Angels Times

The South Korean class warfare thriller is already a massive hit. No disagreement here. — The Chicago Tribune

* destitute: 극빈한(=not having a desirable element)
* searing: 매우 강렬한(=intense), 비판적인(=critical)

< Academy Awards >

The Academy Awards, popularly known as the Oscars, are awards for artistic and technical merit in the film industry. Given annually by the Academy of Motion Picture Arts and Sciences (AMPAS), the awards are an international recognition of excellence in cinematic achievements, as assessed by the Academy's voting membership. The various category winners are awarded a copy of a golden statuette, officially called the "Academy Award of Merit", although more commonly referred to by its nickname, the "**Oscar**". The first Academy Awards ceremony was held on May 16, 1929, at a private dinner function at the Hollywood Roosevelt Hotel with an audience of 270 people. Recipients were announced three months earlier; the next year the Academy kept the results secret but gave an advance list to newspapers for publication at 11 p.m. on the night of the awards. This continued until 1940 when the Los Angeles Times published the winners in its evening edition—readily available to arriving guests. The Academy has, since 1941, used a sealed envelope to reveal the names of the winners.

Dolby Theatre, the venue for the 2020 Academy Awards. 사진: 김경석

The Academy Awards ceremony was first broadcast by radio in 1930 and was first televised in 1953. It is the oldest worldwide entertainment awards ceremony. It is also the oldest of the four major annual American entertainment awards; the Emmy Awards for television, the Tony Awards for theater, and the Grammy Awards for music.

* Oscar: 1939년에 AMPAS에서 공식적으로 이 nickname을 채택했지만, 그 유래는 불확실.

< Oscar statuette facts >

Official Name: Academy Award® of Merit

Height: 13½ inches

Weight: 8½ pounds

Material: The statuettes are solid bronze and plated in 24-karat gold. Due to a metal shortage during World War II, Oscars were made of painted **plaster** for three years. Following the war, the Academy invited recipients to **redeem** the plaster figures for gold-plated metal ones.

source: www.oscar.org

Design:

A stylized figure of a knight holding a crusader's sword standing on a reel of film with five spokes signifying the five original branches of the Academy (actors, directors, producers, technicians and writers). No model was used during the design process.

Designer: Cedric Gibbons, chief art director at Metro-Goldwyn-Mayer

Sculptor: Los Angeles artist George Stanley

Manufacturer: Polich Tallix

Manufacturing Time: 3 months for 50 statuettes

* plaster: 석고

* redeem: 교환하다

세계의 주요 영화제

Name	Place	Founded in	Award for the best film
Cannes Film Festival	Cannes, France	1946	Golden Palm
Venice Film Festival	Venice, Italy	1932	Golden Lion
Berlin International Film Festival	Berlin, Germany	1951	Golden Bear
Toronto International Film Festival	Toronto, Canada	1976	People's Choice Award
Sundance Film Festival	Park City, Utah, US	1978	Grand Jury Prize
Tribeca Film Festival	New York	2002	Best US Narrative Feature/ Best World Narrative Feature
BFI London Film Festival	London	1957	Best Film
Hong Kong International Film Festival	Hong Kong	1976	Firebird Award
Rotterdam Film Festival	Rotterdam, Netherlands	1972	Tiger Award
Edinburgh International Film Festival	Edinburgh, UK	1947	Michael Powell Award for Best British Feature Film/Best International Feature Film
Telluride Film Festival	Telluride, Colorado, US	1974	No category for it.
Chicago International Film Festival	Chicago, US	1964	Golden Hugo
Melbourne International Film Festival	Melbourne, Australia	1952	People's Choice Award for Best Feature
Dubai International Film Festival	Dubai, United Arab Emirates	2004	Best Fiction Feature

Why Korean movie 'Pawn' is the perfect feel-good film to watch this week in the UAE

It's rare to find such cinematic gems that so effectively overcome language barriers to **tug at heartstrings** and draw you in for a long, warm hug. Kang Dae-kyu's 'Pawn' goes down a similar path that was tread in 'Miracle in Cell No 7' to explore the sub-genre of surrogate fathers. While 'Miracle in Cell No 7' saw a group of prisoners raise an inmate's child together, 'Pawn' follows two debt collectors who end up adopting a young child who they had kidnapped as **collateral**. As the film opens in UAE cinemas on July 15, we take a look at why 'Pawn' is the perfect watch with the family over the long Eid Al Adha break.

Kang Dae-kyu is king of compassion

If you've been impressed by director Kang Dae-kyu's 'Harmony', which depicted the tale of inmates with unfortunate stories who find hope through music, then keep those tissues handy before you watch 'Pawn'. In his own words, the award-winning described his work on the movie by saying: "I prepared for 'Pawn' as if I were making a film for the first time. 'Pawn' is like a treasure to me."

Reel Cinema at Dubai Mall. source: www.groupon.ae

* tug/pull at heartstrings: 심금을 울리다(=elicit strong feelings of sympathy)
* collateral: 담보(=a security pledged for the repayment of a loan)

The efforts show in the way Dae-kyu effortlessly weaves humour into some of the most emotionally charged scenes in the film. But the credit really goes to him to make child actress Park Soi, who portrayed the role of nine-year-old Seung-yi, shine on screen in some of the most difficult moments in the film. Speaking about working with Dae-kyu, Park said: "I remember how the director cried with me for an emotional scene," to help her immerse in her role and learn to cry behind the camera for the camera.

Unique story
'Pawn' tells the story of two ruthless **loan sharks** Du-seok (Sung Dong-il) and Jong-bae (Kim Hee-won) who take nine-year-old Seung-yi (Park) as collateral in the hopes of collecting her mother's debt, but **fortuitously** end up raising her. Ha Ji-won, who portrays adult Seung-yi, claimed she was left in tears after reading the screenplay.

* loan shark: 악덕 고리대금업자
* fortuitously: 우연히(=accidentally)

Focus on Grammar

◈ 비제한적 관계절(non-restrictive relative clause)

Ha Ji-won, *who portrays adult Seung-yi*, claimed she was left in tears after reading the screenplay.

비제한적 관계절은 관계대명사 앞의 선행사가 고유명사이거나 혹은 무엇을 지칭하는지 문장을 읽는 사람이 알 것이라는 전제하에 글쓴이가 선행사에 대한 부가적인 정보를 제공하는 표현이다. 관계절 앞에 ,(comma)를 사용하며 관계절이 문장의 중간에 위치하는 경우에는 시작하기 전과 끝에 comma를 사용한다. 위 문장의 경우 선행사가 특정 영화배우이므로 비제한적 관계절을 사용하고 있다. 이러한 원칙을 고려할 때 그 이전 문장은 문법적 오류를 지니고 있다. "... Du-seok (Sung Dong-il) and Jong-bae (Kim Hee-won) who take nine-year-old Seung-yi ..."에서 선행사는 두 주인공으로 글을 읽는 이는 누구를 지칭하는지 알 수 있다. 따라서 관계대명사 앞에 comma를 사용하는 비제한적 관계절이 올바른 표현이다.

"I think the audience will be able to empathise deeply with 'Pawn'. It's a film that is really needed in this day and age," while adding that she decided to take part without hesitation. Sung also added: "I took part in the film with my three children in mind. I can't wait to show it to them. Armed with such lovely and warm charms, 'Pawn' not only promises to bring happy smiles across theatres, but also leave deep impressions with a message that can be shared by all generations."

Cracker of a chemistry
Sung and Kim as the **prickly** retired army officers who become loan sharks are a delight to watch on screen. **Feeding off** each other's **sardonic** sense of humour, the duo perfectly balance out the emotionally heavy moments from 'Pawn'. Explaining their close friendship, Kim says, "I like Sung Dong-il a lot and he likes working with me too. Just like Du-seok and Jong-bae, I like **bantering** with him which came out naturally in the film."

* prickly: 성가신, 골치 아픈(=troublesome)
* feed off: 활용하다
* sardonic: 냉소적인(=mocking, cynical)
* banter: 농담을 주고받다(=tease one another)

◇ 빈 칸에 들어갈 표현을 위 글에서 찾아 문장을 완성해봅시다.

1. The minimum ____________ amount is $5,000 and the maximum will depend on the increase in your home's value.
2. Their ____________ remarks to each of the arguments given by the other teams sent waves of laughter among the crowd.
3. All in all, we understand the emotion of others, and ____________ with them, by invoking the very same neural activity associated with our own emotions.
4. He gained enormous popularity in modernist circles due to his ____________ and to his effective peace-making activities.
5. I'm hoping that sleeping in tomorrow will ____________ all of my late nights this week.

A star is born

Child actress Park Soi is the surprise package of the film. Bringing innocent humour to her character, Park manages to defer from the **cloying** sweetness that child stars are expected to **emote** on screen. Her confidence, just with a hint of **sass**, puts her miles ahead of the competition and a sure-fire force to reckon with in Korean film and TV.

According to the makers, Park was selected out of a shortlist of 300 hopefuls **vying** for the role. If she looks familiar, it is possible you saw her shine as Yoo-min in '**Deliver Us from Evil**'.

'Pawn' director Kang spoke highly of her, saying: "She is an actress who is well aware of the situation and gets instantly immersed in her role really well. She has great concentration and energy. Her beautiful eyes will attract audiences and keep them glued to her throughout the film."

At a time when cinemas are bracing for superhero adventures and action **tentpoles**, this small film is all heart and definitely worth a watch over the Eid Al Adha break with your children **in tow**. 'Pawn' releases in UAE cinemas on July 15. The film is in Korean with English subtitles.

* cloying: 질릴 정도의(=initially pleasurable or sweet but wearying in excess)
* emote: 감정을 지나치게 표현하다(=express emotion in an excessive manner)
* sass: 건방진 말투나 행동(=disrespectful talk or behaviour)
* vie: 경쟁하다. 과거/과거분사형 vied, 현재분사형 vying
* Deliver Us From Evil: 황정민, 이정재 주연의 2020년도 영화 '다만 악에서 구하소서'
* in tow: 데리고(=accompanying alongside)

"Focus on Terminology"

◆ tentpole/tent pole

미디어 산업에서 자주 사용하는 용어인 tentpole은, 텐트를 세울 때 중앙의 튼튼한 기둥이 텐트 전체를 지탱하는데 큰 역할을 하는 것에 비유하여 다음을 의미 한다: 'a large-scale entertainment production that is a major source of revenue for its studio, television network, or investors and its earnings are expected to compensate for their less profitable productions'

연관된 표현으로는,

- hammock: 한 tv 방송사에서 두 개의 tentpole series를 가지고 있을 때 두 프로그램을 연이어 방송하지 않고, 중간에 다소 인기가 없거나 신생 프로그램을 끼워 넣어 시청률을 높이는 전략을 사용하는데 이 프로그램을 hammock이라 부른다.
- four-quadrant movie: 영화 관객들을 인구학적(demographic)으로 크게 네 부류로 나누고 그들 모두를 만족 시킬 수 있는 영화를 의미한다.

남성. 25세 이하	여성. 25세 이하
남성. 25세 이상	여성. 25세 이상

◆ 최고 수익 영화 목록 vs. inflation을 반영한 최고 수익 영화 목록 (2020 기준)

1	Avatar	$2,847,246,203	Gone with the Wind*	$3,739,000,000
2	Avengers: Endgame	$2,797,501,328	Avatar	$3,286,000,000
3	Titanic	$2,187,425,379	Titanic	$3,108,000,000
4	Star Wars: The Force Awakens	$2,068,223,624	Star Wars	$3,071,000,000
5	Avengers: Infinity War	$2,048,359,754	Avengers: Endgame	$2,823,000,000
6	Jurassic World	$1,671,713,208	The Sound of Music**	$2,572,000,000
7	The Lion King	$1,656,943,394	E.T.	$2,511,000,000
8	The Avengers	$1,518,812,988	The Ten Commandments	$2,377,000,000
9	Furious 7	$1,516,045,911	Doctor Zhivago	$2,253,000,000
10	Frozen II	$1,450,026,933	Star Wars: The Force Awakens	$2,221,000,000

* 1939년에 개봉 ** 1965년에 개봉 source: www.boxofficemojo.com

Pawn 관람 후기

Although the story of this movie is fairly simple without much plot twist, the movie is actually heartwarming and engaging to watch, probably due to the convincing acting from the movie cast. Both young and older Seung-yi seemed really close to Doo-seok and Jong-bae, and the relationship between Doo-seok and Jong-bae was similar to Song Dong-il and Kim Hee-won in *House on Wheels*. I would recommend this movie to watch, especially if you have spare time as it is easy and comfortable to watch.

* House on Wheels: 영화 '바퀴 달린 집'

I don't shed a tear when I watch movie these days maybe I became cold hearted or growing up has changed me watching this world going into eternal burning of hatred sideways. This movie made me emotional.

This movie was splendid. I literally wept out my eyes watching it. Truly, not blood relations are all relations. In fact emotions like love, affection, care compassion are some of the terms we truly understand when we make friends with different people to whom we are not at all related. I have watched Sung dong il in many other series and movies but this one was the best of his collections.

It was a simple cute story with twist and turns that no one would have guessed for this age—always thought something bad would happen. A debt collector who is kind, a hostess who is not that-much of an evil stepmom, the kid was never arrogant when she grew up or wished to go back to her parents. Something not-so-ordinary to come across in a movie.

10/10 or rather a trillion times more. What a LOVE, a fatherly love to a child. It started wrong yes, just like we all had that started wrong but it will NEVER dent an immeasurable LOVE of a father as portrayed in this movie. I just wonder for other fathers that never cared out there. I love my kids!!!

I just bawled my eyes out as I watched this movie. The compassion of the characters, the comic timing, and the innocence of the child created a true master piece and a treat for a viewer's eyes! This movie shows perfectly that not all people with sweet words are good and not all people who are deemed to have no moral are evil.

* bawl: 울어대다

The 10 Best Korean Zombie Movies to Sink Your Teeth Into

The Korean film industry is experiencing something of a zombie resurrection. While all eyes are on the international success of addictive K-dramas and Bong Joon-ho's Academy Award-winning film *Parasite*, the country's filmmakers are also creating some of the most ambitious, **unsettling** and even comedic entries to the zombie genre. The renewed K-zombie movie trend arguably began with Yeon Sang-ho's 2016 *Train to Busan*, which envisions a zombie outbreak on a moving train—and has since expanded to encompass many more films.

Perhaps most interesting about Korean zombie movies is how the **apocalyptic** visions offer a dash of social criticism—hitting at the rigidity of class structures, the **encroachment** of technological advances, or the collapse of society after the random introduction of a viral **pathogen**. Essentially, these Korean movies aren't all just made to get easy scares from flesh eating monsters.

From Netflix's newly released *#Alive* to *Peninsula*, these zombie movies have a little bit of everything—psychological thrillers, body horror, class **allegories**, and even a historical drama, all unified under their shared subject matter: the undead.

* unsettling: 불안하게 만드는(=disturbing, disruptive)
* apocalyptic: 종말론적(=prophetic of devastation or ultimate doom)
* encroachment: 침입(=any entry into an area not previously occupied)
* pathogen: 병원균
* allegory: 풍자

“ Focus on Vocabulary ”

◆ sink one's teeth into

'몰입하다' '열중하다' 뜻(become fully engaged/engrossed)을 지닌 숙어 표현. 원래는 동물이 먹이 속으로 이를 깊숙이 넣고 먹는 모습을 묘사하는 표현이었는데, 어떤 일에 집중하는 비유적 의미를 가지게 됨. 예) She is always looking for a great book to sink her teeth into.

1. ***Train to Busan*** (2016)

If you're a horror movie **aficionado**, you've likely heard of the box office and critical hit *Train to Busan*. The Gong Woo-led movie follows a group of travelers fighting for their lives aboard a zombie-infested high-speed train **hurtling** to one of the last safe places in the country. The film's powerful class commentary shows the benefit of taking collective action over prioritizing individual survival.

2. ***Peninsula*** (2020)

This *Train to Busan* sequel picks up where the **seminal** film left off. While *Peninsula* isn't jam-packed with the social analysis that fans of the first film praised, it does feature the kind of body horror that fans of the genre know and love. This time, the survivors of the zombie apocalypse in the Korean Peninsula are safe and sound in Hong Kong. That is, until Jung-seok (played by Gang Dong Won) gets caught up in a scheme to recover $20 million back in Seoul. Yeon Sang-ho returns to direct this hybrid zombie-heist thriller, choosing to wander through the **eerie** CGI post-apocalyptic wasteland that has few human survivors.

source: www.theface.com

* aficionado: 열렬한 애호가(=fan, enthusiast)

* hurtle: 돌진하다(=rush, race)

* seminal: 최초의(=original) cf. 글에서 the seminal film은 *Train to Busan*을 지칭

* eerie: 섬뜩한(=uncanny), 기괴한

3. ***#Alive*** **(2020)**
The definitive quarantine film that was somehow conceived before the pandemic Il Cho's *#Alive* follows a **spacey** gamer who is stuck in the house while a **zombie apocalypse** rages at his doorstep. He's running out of food, and it's not like zombies give up on a siege. As the days pass and the situation continues to devolve into the end of times, he makes contact with a neighbor and together they plot their escape.

Here is the rest of the list.
4. *The Wailing* (2016)
5. *Seoul Station* (2016)
6. *The Odd Family: Zombie on Sale* (2019)
7. *Doomsday Book* (2012)
8. *Rampant* (2018)
9. *Horror Stories* (2012)
10. *The Guard Post* (2008)

* spacey: 이상한, 별난(=eccentric)
* zombie apocalypse: 좀비에 감염된 사람

< More info on the rest of the list >

	우리말 제목	주연 배우
4. The Wailing	곡성	곽도원, 황정민, 천우희
5. Seoul Station	서울역	류승룡, 심은경, 이준
6. The Odd Family: Zombie on Sale	기묘한 가족	정재영, 김남길, 엄지원
7. Doomsday Book	인류멸망보고서	김강우, 송영창, 김규리
8. Rampant	창궐	현빈, 장동건, 조우진
9. Horror Stories	무서운 이야기	김지영, 정은채, 김현수
10. The Guard Post	GP506	천호진, 조현재, 이영훈

◇ 아래에 주어진 단어들을 활용하거나, 괄호 안 단어를 활용하여 적절한 표현으로 빈 칸을 채워봅시다.

fast-paced rise stepping alike instability feeding

The rise of K-zombie entertainment has produced action-packed horror movies that have **enthralled** local and international audiences __________. So, what exactly makes these Korean zombie movies so popular? Victoria Kim, the Seoul correspondent for the Los Angeles Times, writes that zombies in Korean television and movies are "__________ on fears and anxieties" in South Korea. Much like how post-apocalyptic stories often reflect uncertainties about the present, the K-zombie trend speaks to __________ (linger) fears about crisis management, hunger, financial __________, and upper-class privilege, as well as the stress of keeping up with a __________, competitive society.
Consider the Korean zombie thriller *#Alive*, which within two days of international release climbed to the __________ (high) spot on Netflix as the most-streamed movie in 35 countries. It follows Joon-woo, a young gamer who finds himself __________ (trap) in his apartment when a zombie epidemic overtakes Seoul. When Joon-woo runs out of the basic **amenities** in his apartment, he must venture out into streets that are **festering** with **ravenous** brain-eaters. *#Alive*'s similarities to the COVID-19 pandemic can't __________ (ignore). Everyone is familiar with the slow-building dread of quarantine, the perils of __________ outside, and the paranoia of not __________ (know) who has been infected by the virus. But it's not all doom and gloom: Korean zombie movies can also depict how mankind might unite and __________ above the toughest crisis.

* enthrall: 마음을 사로잡다(=captivate)
* amenity: 생활 편의 물건(=something that contributes to comfort)
* fester: 곪아터지다, 부패하다(=decay)
* ravenous: 굶주린, 포식성의(=predatory)

한국 영화의 영어 제목

외국에 영화를 수출할 때 제목을 글자 그대로 번역하는 경우도 있지만, 때론 전혀 다른 영어 제목을 사용하는 경우도 있다. 다음은 각각 어떤 영화의 제목인지 알아 맞혀봅시다.

영어 제목	개봉 연도	주연 배우	우리말 제목
Snowpiercer	2013	송강호, Jacques Lob	
Ode to My Father	2014	황정민, 김윤진, 정진영	
The Age of Shadows	2016	송강호, 공유, 한지민	
Midnight Runners	2017	박서준, 강하늘	
The Battleship Island	2017	황정민, 소지섭, 이정현	
Intimate Strangers	2018	유해진, 조진웅, 이서진	
There is no way out!	2019	윤아, 조정석	
The Man Standing Next	2020	이병헌, 이성민, 곽도원	
Space Sweepers	2021	송중기, 김태리, 진선규	
	2012	이제훈, 수지, 조정석	건축학개론
	2014	심은경, 나문희	수상한 그녀
	2016	황정민, 강동원	검사외전
	2017	현빈, 유해진, 김주혁	공조
	2017	마동석, 윤계상	범죄도시
	2018	하정우, 주지훈, 김향기	신과함께: 인과 연
	2019	류승룡, 이하늬, 진선규	극한직업
	2020	이제훈, 안재홍, 최우식	사냥의 시간
	2021	김윤석, 허준호, 조인성	모가디슈

영국과 미국의 영화 rating system

U PG 12A 12 15 18

U	Universal. Suitable for all ages.
PG	Parental guidance suggested. Suitable for ages 8 and above.
12A	People under 12 must be accompanied by an adult.
12	No one under 12 is admitted.
15	No one under 15 is admitted.
18	No one under 18 is admitted.

UK film classification. source: www.bbfc.co.uk

G	General Audiences. All ages permitted
PG	Parental Guidance Suggested. Some material may not be suitable for children.
PG-13	Parents Strongly Cautioned. Some material may be inappropriate for children under 13.
R	Restricted. Under 17 requires accompanying parent or adult guardian.
NC-17	Adults Only. No One 17 and Under Admitted. Clearly adult. Children are not admitted.

US film rating system. source: www.motionpictures.org

참고: 1990년에 16세 이하는 관람할 수 없는 NC-17 rating이 처음 생겼는데, 1996년에 들어서 17세 이하는 관람을 금지하도록 나이 제한을 상향함.

< Famous Quotes About Movies >

I want to move people, stir something within them that makes them feel. That's what a movie should do and an actor should do, make you feel something. I think that's why people love films so much. — Nadine Velazquez

People only rooted for the underdog in movies, not in middle school. — David Wright

Film-makers are always going to be interested in making movies that plug into society around them. That's what a vibrant, artistically alert community should be doing. After all, it would be sad if we only made films about alien robots. — Mark Boal

I grew up in Europe, and I used to like those very slow-moving European films. I've been contaminated by the American TV culture, and I just want things to move faster now. — Rebecca De Mornay

Movies were never an art form, they were entertainment. It just evolved into an art form from there, and it's still evolving in different ways. — David Mamet

In all of the movies you see, people are always in crisis because that's what we watch. We watch them deal with crisis and resolve it. — Julianne Moore

When women get great roles in life, they start to get great roles in films and TV. Look at Janet Reno, Madeleine Albright, and Mrs. Thatcher. Because those images are coming at us in life, they are reflected in acting. — Helen Mirren

I like crime movies where the crime is so incredible that, attractive as it seems, you don't wanna do it because it's just too dangerous. — Ice-T

I was lucky that I made a few movies in a row that people really responded to—not me, particularly, but the films as a whole were appreciated. — Julia Roberts

I love horror movies and I love being scared, but I don't like them, if they're not based on a true story. It's like knowing how the sausage is made. — Olivia Munn

Cross-word Puzzle

ACROSS

1. disrespectful talk
3. extremely painful
6. cynically mocking
8. to become worse or rotten
9. a person or thing that indicates a trend
11. to strive for victory
12. extremely poor
13. to capture the fascinated attention of
15. an enthusiastic admirer or follower
16. to tease one another

DOWN

2. a person who victimizes others
4. to gain entrance secretly
5. making one feel rather worried
7. highly original
10. to display exaggerated emotion
14. to turn in and receive something in exchange

Chapter IV

K-FOOD

Foodies across the globe are taking part in the 'fire noodle challenge'

The noodle, officially called buldak ramen, became popular in Seoul after YouTube users took on the "fire noodle challenge," which requires a person to consume the incredibly spicy food as fast as possible. The noodle's chewy texture reminds Koreans of topokki, a snack food made of rice cake and hot pepper paste. There are more than a million videos on YouTube of people trying the fire noodle challenge. Some are **gasping for air**, running for a glass of water or even crying after tasting the hot and delicious instant noodle.

source: www.amazon.com

"I love buldak ramen because we don't have anything like it in the states," Angela Chun told ABC News. "The buldak ramen has this burning sensation in my mouth which I was **mesmerized** by." The notorious buldak ramen made its debut in the instant noodle market in 2012, targeting spicy food lovers.

Kim Jung-soo, president of Samyang Food, the maker of buldak ramen, said two tons of sauce and over a thousand chickens were used to develop the recipe.

* foodie: 음식에 열정적 관심을 가진 사람(=foodist)
* gasp for air: 숨을 헉헉거리다(=breathe noisily, pant, puff)
* mesmerize: (자석처럼) 마음을 끌다(=magnetize, bewitch, attract strongly)

Then the company targeted "young and **audacious** people who would challenge themselves with spicy instant noodle for fun," Won Joo-yeon, who leads the instant ramen soup team for Samyang Food, told ABC News. To keep up with consumer demand, Samyang Food is constantly trying different variations from its original version, such as cheese, curry, mala and carbonara. One of the variations, "extremely spicy buldak ramen," has earned the title of the spiciest instant noodle sold in the market.

* audacious: 대담한(=extremely daring, bold, fearless, brave)

3X Spicy Buldak Ramen (3배 매운 불닭볶음면)에 대한 reactions

- Awesome! I hope to find it at some point in the future. My body says 'NO' but my mind says "**** Yeah" with spicy foods.
- I've eaten these recently, they are the hottest noodles I've ever eaten.
- Damn I didn't know there was an 3x, I gotta get some to try it.
- I eat this dry just the sauce on the noodles without the water, and it's burning hot that way. lol
- I will never ever buy the 3x ever again.
- My lips and tongue were super red and swollen because of the spice level, it is really very very spicy, for people with low spice tolerance, don't try it out cuz all you will feel is spice and nothing else. No taste nothing, just burning.
- This product has no flavor whatsoever except very hot taste. You'd not get anything except the stingy hot sensation. It's like having a very bitter black coffee without any extra taste.
- I tried these and I only cried twice, once when I was eating them, and again in the bathroom.
- Sometimes when I eat spicy noodles, I blow on them thinking it'll change the spiciness of the noodles.
- Bought it yesterday, I'm scared to eat this.
- instant noodles for instant regret.

Focus on Terminology

◈ spicy food 관련 표현들

- addictive: 중독성이 있는. 예) Unlike chemicals like alcohol and caffeine, hot sauce isn't chemically addictive.
- burn off: (에너지, 칼로리를) 다 사용하다. 예) Cayenne pepper, a key ingredient in curries, raises body temperature and helps you burn off calories
- cyclically spicy food: 매운 맛을 진정시키기 위해서 계속해서 먹게 되는 매운 음식.
- kick: 강한 맛. 예) The food is fresh and the hot sauce has a kick which makes me happy.
- neutralize: 중화시키다. 상쇄시키다. 예) Adding a small amount of sugar is a great way to neutralize the spiciness of noodles.
- numb: 감각이 없는. 예) I've had my face feel a bit numb after eating really spicy food.
- pungent: 톡 쏘는(=tangy). 예) White pepper has a smoother skin and slightly less pungent taste than black pepper.
- relieve: 진정시키다. 예) When you eat spicy food, drinking cool water can help relieve the feeling that you just swallowed a fireball.
- sweat: 땀을 흘리다. 예) After eating hot and spicy foods, some people sweat from the face—the lips, forehead, nose, and scalp.
- take the roof of your mouth off (=burn your mouth with spicy food) 입천장을 데일 정도로 음식이 매움을 비유적으로 표현.
- tingle: (혀가) 얼얼하다. 예) If you like to feel your mouth tingle with spice, the hot pepper indicator on the menu will help your choice.
- ulcer: 궤양. 예) The spicy food might aggravate the ulcer, but it doesn't cause it. 참고로, 매운 음식이 위궤양(stomach ulcer)을 초래한다는 대중적인 믿음과는 달리 요즘의 많은 연구들은 둘 사이에 상관관계가 없음을 보여주고 있다(https://www.uchicagomedicine.org/forefront/health-and-wellness-articles/spicy-foods-healthy-or-dangerous).
- urge (=crave for): (~이) 당기다. 예) The restaurant is highly recommended if you have the urge for some nice spicy food.

◇ 다음 단어들을 사용하여 빈 칸을 채워봅시다.

hit translates viral variations portfolio released marinated foray doubles challenge explosive

South Korean spicy ramen craze continues, halal version to be launched in Indonesia

When Samyang Foods ___________ Buldak Spicy Chicken Ramen in 2012, the company did not expect it would receive such ___________ popularity from customers abroad—especially in the YouTube community. Buldak refers to grilled chicken ___________ in super-spicy red chilli paste. Its name ___________ to "fire chicken". It remains unknown where the meat dish originated, but it became popular among South Koreans in the early 2000s. In 2014, a British YouTuber called "Korean Englishman" uploaded a video in which he filmed reactions of foreigners trying the Buldak ramen. Most of those brave souls could not bear the spiciness of the noodles. The video soon went ___________ and since then, numerous YouTubers have taken on the ___________ of eating it, dubbing it the "fire noodles challenge".

Buoyed by the unprecedented popularity, Samyang Foods began releasing different ___________ of the Buldak series: Cheese Buldak Ramen, Mara Buldak Ramen, Curry Buldak Ramen and Carbo Buldak Ramen, to mention a few. In 2017, Haek Buldak Extra Spicy Chicken Ramen, which measures 8,000 Scoville Heat Units, ___________ the local market. It ___________ the spiciness of the original one. Having successfully expanded its sales ___________ across the globe including the United States, Europe, Australia and South-east Asia, Samyang now plans to make an aggressive ___________ into the Halal market. Halal-certified Buldak ramen will be available in Indonesia starting in late 2018.

* foray: 새로운 영역에 도전, 급습(=sudden raid)

* buoyed: 고무되어(=encouraged, inspired, elevated, elated)

Scoville Heat Unit

고추의 매운 맛(spiciness 또는 heat) 정도를 나타내는 것으로, 캡사이신(capsaicin)의 농도를 단위로 표시. 1912년 미국의 약사인 Wilbur Scoville이 창안.

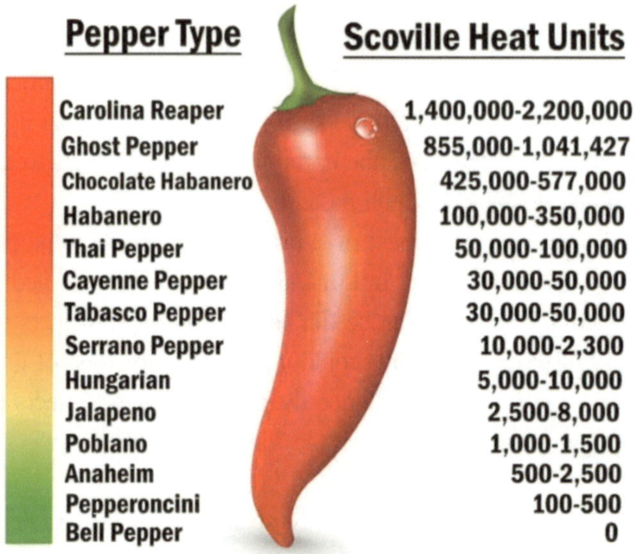

source: www.ebay.com

- Carolina Reaper: South Carolina의 Ed Currie가 개발한 품종.
- Ghost pepper: 인도 남동부에서 재배되는 고추.
- Habanero: 남미에서 재배되는 고추. 멕시코 유카탄 반도가 최대 생산지.
- Chocolate Habanero: 초콜릿색을 띈 Habanero.
- Cayenne pepper: 프랑스령 Guiana에서 유래한 것으로 알려짐.
- Tabasco pepper: 멕시코의 Tabasco 지역에서 유래.
- Serrano pepper: 멕시코의 Puebla와 Hildalgo 지역의 산맥에서 재배.
- Jalapeno: 멕시코의 Jalapa (=Xalapa) 지역에서 유래.
- Poblano: 멕시코의 Puebla 지역에서 유래.
- Pepperoncini: 이탈리아 남부에서 재배되는 고추.
- Bell pepper: bell 모양의 고추로, 지역에 따라서는 파프리카(paprika)로 부름.

How a Korean restaurant owner thrives in Halifax during the pandemic

When the pandemic first started in March, Joungmin Kim, like many other restaurant owners in Halifax, thought his business would **hobble** over for a few months **at best**, if not be closed. He had just opened a new location on Dutch Village Road in April and was "panicking" about the future of his new investment. Yet nine months after the city's first lockdown, Kim's restaurant, Backoos Korean To Go Food, is still **afloat** and expanding. Sales have gone up by 25 to 30 per cent, according to Kim. And he is hiring four more people to work at one of his three restaurants located in downtown Halifax. "Once you have convenience, which is delivery, then you have the quality that's the same as dining in, you will just enjoy it so much. That's what happened in South Korea and China," said Kim.

source: Backoos Korean Food's Instagram

* thrive: 번창하다(=prosper, boom)
* hobble: 절뚝거리다
* at best: 잘해야, 기껏(=in the best possible scenario)
* afloat: 망하지 않은(=in business), 빚이 없는

Kim opened his restaurant with insights and knowledge from the food delivery industry in South Korea, which has been around for more than 50 years. The menus are the same across the three restaurants, as is the quality. The variety on the menu is limited with almost only **staple** food and fried chicken, but Kim is **meticulous** in making sure the quality. "It is really important when people see it and open it and food is organized and looks good," said Kim.

Kim said his special way of packing the chicken will keep the air inside and make sure that when the customer opens the box, the food looks fresh—another lesson he learned from unsuccessful restaurants in South Korea's food delivery industry.

* staple: 기본적인(=principle, main), 중요한
* meticulous: 꼼꼼한, 철저한(=thorough, painstaking)

"Focus on Grammar"

◈ 주어와 동사의 도치(inversion)

The menus are the same across the three restaurants, *as is the quality*.

두 번째 절에서 동사이하의 표현이 앞 절의 그 것과 동일한 경우에 생략을 하고 as이하를 도치한 구문이다. 위 문장은 '메뉴가 3개의 식당에서 같은 것처럼, 품질도 3개의 식당에서 동일하다'는 의미이므로 as이하에서 주어와 동사를 도치하였다.

- Italy produces many excellent wines, as does Spain.
- France is a founder member of the EU, as is Belgium.

두 개의 절로 이루어진 문장에서 두 번째 절에 도치를 사용하는 가장 흔한 경우는 부정적 의미를 지닌 접속사로 두 번째 절이 시작하는 경우이다.

- The house has no central heating, nor does it have a boiler.
- I never learned to swim and neither did she.

"Our delivery system was there for 50 years. We've had times when the food (delivery) was bad. But then a lot of companies (in South Korea) now know how to make the food look like they were five minutes ago at the restaurant," said Kim. What Kim is doing is nothing new in his home country. Food delivery has been around in South Korea since 1930 and has recently experienced a boom due to COVID-19. South Korea's food delivery market is expected to jump 40 per cent this year to around $15.4 billion from $11 billion in 2019, according to market researcher Euromonitor's data, topped only by China and the United States.

source: www.foodora.com

Halifax. source: www.google.com/maps

Every morning Kim will come to each location, hours before the restaurant is open, to make sure the material is fresh enough and the restaurant is ready to start the day. He spends **generously** on food ingredients such as chicken and pepper. Kim said the process of making the chicken, from **marinating** to frying not once but twice, can take up to 36 hours. "We always wanted to do this to really high standards. We're really careful because that could really hurt me, hurt business and people," said Kim. A box of Korean fried chicken can cost less than $25 plus delivery fees, using any delivery app Backoos is on.

Kim came to Halifax seven years ago with his wife, who is originally from Nova Scotia. He had a business in South Korea where he owned a bar and a restaurant. Kim thought opening a restaurant that has the most popular comfort food from his hometown seemed like a low-risk option. Kim then asked his friend, Jean Pierre Hong, who is a celebrity chef in Sydney, Australia, to come up with the secret recipe and started his small bistro in downtown Halifax. Now the business has expanded to three different locations and is thriving during the pandemic. Kim said he's planning to open another location in the coming year. "Right now it's local. But we want to branch out nationally and internationally," said Kim.

* generously: (보통 사람들이 생각하는 것 보다) 아낌없이 돈을 지불하는(=in a way that shows willingness to give a lot of money than expected)
* marinate: 양념장에 재워두다

"Focus on Terminology"

◈ Marinade (양념장)

고기나 생선을 재울 때 어떤 성분을 활용하느냐에 따라 양념장은 크게 다음 세 가지로 나뉜다.

1. acidic marinade: 포도주, 식초, 또는 토마토/오렌지/레몬 등의 산성을 활용
2. dairy marinade: 칼슘 성분으로 숙성시키는 것으로 우유, 요거트 등을 활용
3. enzyme marinade: 키위, 파파야, 파인애플 등에 있는 효소의 효과를 활용

Focus on Grammar

◆ 분사구문

A box of Korean fried chicken can cost less than $25 plus delivery fees, *using any delivery app Backoos is on*.

분사구문은 시간(~할 때, ~하는 동안에, ~와 동시에), 이유(~ 때문에), 양보(~임에도 불구하고), 조건(~하면, ~를 고려할 때) 등을 나타내는 부사절의 역할을 한다. 위 밑줄 친 부분에서는 '조건'을 나타내는데, 'Backoos (식당 이름)가 입점한 배달앱을 사용하면(if you use any delivery app Backoos is on)'을 의미한다. 다양한 부사절의 의미를 지닌 분사구문의 예는 다음과 같다.

1. 시간
- Hearing the good news, she wanted to cry. ~할 때
- Drinking his coffee slowly, he thought about the problem. ~하면서

2. 이유
- Feeling sick, David left school early.
- Having an assignment to finish, I cannot come with you.

3. 양보
- Being very popular, he was frequently criticised for his self-centered attitude.
- Granting you were drunk, I cannot excuse you.

4. 조건
- Getting off at the third stop, you'll find the library.
- Taking this medicine as prescribed, you'll get better soon.

◇ 각 문장에서 분사구문은 시간, 이유, 양보, 조건 부사절 중 어떤 역할을 하는가?

a. Not having had any breakfast, I was very hungry. ____________
b. Living next door to him, I don't know him well. ____________
c. Doing the high jump, the athlete twisted her ankle. ____________
d. Being a kind person, she agreed to help us. ____________
e. The child sat at the desk painting a picture. ____________
f. Not studying harder, you'll fail to pass the exam. ____________

피자를 주문하면서 delivery service app에 남긴 재미있는 요구 사항

- Crust a little crisper than normal. But not too crispy. If that's not vague enough, make it like you're taking revenge on a cheating boyfriend, but you still want to reconcile in the not so distant future.
- When you approach house, turn off car lights, don't ring door bell or knock. Walk to the garage and start humming the batman theme song.
- My coworker and I are both working double shifts and this pizza will be the only thing getting us through it. Can you give us some extra motivation/inspiration? Also, you guys are awesome. ⇒ 동료와 주문자 둘 다 밤낮으로 근무하고 있는데 피자가 힘든 시간을 견디도록 도움을 준다고 말하면서, 동기부여를 해달라고 요청함(서비스로 뭔가 추가로 달라는 암시).
- Please draw a self-portrait on the box.
- Draw a dragon fighting a flamingo.
- Draw a snowman on the box.

source: www.delish.com

- Go up to the second window left of the door and I will retrieve there because I don't want the people in my living room knowing about the pizza cuz I don't wanna share.
- In your best opera voice, sing the pizza is here as loudly as possible!
- Please can you write a silly joke on the pizza? My 6-year-old kid loves jokes and is feeling unwell :) Thanks

Kimchi is Giving Classic American Food a New Kick

Traditionally its own side dish on the Korean peninsula, kimchi's day has arrived in America thanks to a number of chefs who have been finding new uses for the **fermented** vegetables that come out of the jar tasting like sauerkraut's spicy and sour cousin from another continent, namely by dumping a couple of hearty **dollops** of it on top of some of our favorite comfort foods.

While there are over 80 varieties of kimchi, as recorded by the Kimchi Field Museum, the most familiar variety is tongbaechu-kimchi, or the traditional, spicy **Napa cabbage kimchi**. It's made with hot pepper flakes, **scallions**, ginger, Korean radish, and fish sauce, among other ingredients. But since the first thing somebody might notice is the strong-smell, kimchi and Korean food in general hasn't quite become as popular as other Asian cuisines, like Japanese sushi or **pad thai** from Thailand.

* fermented: 발효시킨
* dollop [ˈdɑːləp]: 소량, 약간
* Napa cabbage kimchi: 우리가 흔히 포기김치(poki kimchi)라 부르는 것. tongbaechu kimchi와 혼용함.
* scallion: 파. green onion이라고도 함.
* pad thai: 달걀, 타마린, 땅콩, 새우, 콩나물 등이 들어간 볶은 쌀국수

“Focus on Terminology”

◆ Kick

깜짝 놀라게 하는 것/즐거운 자극(pleasurable stimulation)을 뜻하는데, 음식에 대해서 이야기 할 때는 강한 맛(strong flavor) 그중에서도 특히 매운 맛을 표현할 때 사용한다. 어떤 음식이 생각보다 매울 때 'have a kick to it (them)' 숙어를 사용한다. 예를 들어, Those chicken wings are supposed to be mild, but they really have a kick to them. 위 숙어는 주류에 생각한 것보다 많은 알콜이 함유되었을 때도 사용한다: 예, That drink has a real kick to it—I'll be drunk in another three sips!

One of its most recent boosters was **Umami** Burger, which opened its third New York City location in March of this year. As part of opening in the hip Williamsburg neighborhood of Brooklyn that's already **brimming** with restaurants to compete with, Umami Burger unveiled the K-BBQ, short for the Korean Barbecue Burger. Created by their executive chef Ted Hopson, and topped with a caramelized cabbage-based kimchi and the almost equally pungent gochujang glaze. The result is a burger with a flavor that's **tangy**, but sweet, not quite the spiciness I expected. According to general manager Alex Adelman, so far it's a **fan favorite**. "It was the right place to debut our K-BBQ burger," he noted, as the burger is exclusively offered in the Williamsburg location for now, with plans to expand the offering to all Umami locations.

Umami Burger isn't the first to introduce kimchi to the customer's **palate** by pairing it with more familiar flavors. Korean-American author Alexander Chee cited a **who's who list** of Korean American chefs who have worked to introduce Korean food to America over email, including Jenny Kwak and her mom Myung Ja Kwak, Roy Choi, David Chang and Hooni Kim. "They have all done more to **mainstream** those flavors than anyone else," he added. "In particular, Roy is the one who made Korean tacos a thing, which happened pretty much as a relationship between him and the Mexican food and Mexican American people around him in Los Angeles."

* umami: 이 글에서는 고유명사로 사용되고 있는데, '맛있는'을 뜻하는 일본어이다.
* tangy: 톡 쏘는
* fan favorite: 지역 명물(=local celebrity)
* palate: 미각
* who's who list: 유명인사 목록
* mainstream (v): 주류에 편입시키다

Focus on Vocabulary

◈ brim

명사로서 brim은 컵 같은 용기의 상단 끝 부분을 가리키는데, 이 글에서는 '(새로 개업한 지역이) 경쟁해야 할 식당들로 꽉 차있다(=be completely full)'는 동사이다.

Chef Phil Lee has done similar work in Brooklyn since 2011 with his Kimchi Taco Truck. "My personal goal as a Korean American has always been to popularize Korean food in America by making it more accessible to Americans who never tried or **turned off** because of its strong flavors," he explained over email. Lee decided to pair kimchi with tacos and other '**street classics**' like burritos and falafel. For him, it's a matter of introducing foods like kimchi **in a subtle way**, such as a topping on a taco. It's all about small steps. Lee compared it to approaching sushi for the first time: "You don't just start with **uni** or sashimi but you graduate from cucumber rolls to California rolls." There's a level of **guidance necessary**, and Lee is more than happy to provide it with his Kimchi Taco Truck, and now his restaurant Kimchi Grill with two Brooklyn locations.

* turn off: 관심을 끊다
* street classic: 대표적인 길거리 음식
* in a subtle way: (양이나 변화가 매우 작아) 알아차리기 힘들게
* uni: '성게'를 뜻하는 일본어
* guidance necessary: 필요한 안내지침. 'There's a level of guidance necessary'는 한국 음식을 처음 접하는 사람들에게 어떤 음식부터 시도하고 차츰 익숙해지면 시도할 음식의 단계가 있다는 의미.

Kimchi Taco Truck. source: www.newyorkstreetfood.com

The main key to kimchi's recent success has been introducing kimchi as an "additive" to dishes customers are already familiar with, but there's also the health benefits, as Kimchi Grill's site notes: vitamin A and C, carotene thiamine (B1), riboflavin (B2), calcium, and iron, along with healthy bacteria, similar to the kind in yogurt. As Americans begin to **gravitate** towards more healthy foods, this positive tendency opens **culinary**, and culture, doors.

kimchi taco. source: www.bodhiboxmarket.com

While other internationally-born sides like hummus or guacamole have become popular in America in recent years, kimchi **renders** those almost subtle in comparison, it's a more complex and ultimately difficult taste and smell to get used to. Somebody who grew up with it around, Chee finds humor in the current popularity of kimchi: "I remember my dad trying to take a big barrel of it into Canada to give to some friends, and the customs officials made him open it. They had opened it because he had said 'Don't open that!'

* gravitate: 끌리다(=be attracted to)
* culinary: 요리의
* render: ~하게 만들다. 'kimchi renders those almost subtle in comparison'은 '김치는 (맛이나 냄새가 매우 독특한 튀는 음식이어서) hummus나 guacamole 같은 음식들을 비교적 두드러지지 않는 음식으로 생각하게 한다'는 의미.

Then they wanted to throw it out, because of the smell, and he kept saying 'No, no, it's supposed to smell like this.'" Eventually, his father was allowed to bring it with him as the customs officials "evacuated the building because of the smell." He's glad to see Americans embracing kimchi, but he said the real test of liking it is if you'll have it with your breakfast food to really call yourself a **connoisseur**.

* connoisseur: 전문가(=a person of informed and discriminating taste)

Focus on Grammar

◈ 가능성을 나타내는 'if' 그리고 'to-부정사'의 부사적 용법

... but he said the real test of liking it is *if* you'll have it with your breakfast food *to really call yourself a connoisseur*.

이 문장의 뜻은, '그가 말하길 그 것(김치)을 좋아하는지 잘 알아보는 방법으로 당신을 진정으로 (김치의 맛을 아는) 전문가로 부를 수 있을 정도로 아침 식사에 김치를 포함하는지 여부이다.'

a. 문장에서 if의 경우 두 가지 가능성(~ 인지 아닌지=whether)을 언급하는 접속사로 사용되고 있다. 가장 보편적인 '조건'을 언급하는 접속사와 용법상의 다른 점은 시제의 사용에 있다. 'If-조건절'의 경우 미래 상황을 언급할 때 '현재 시제'를 사용하지만, 위처럼 가능성을 언급하는 의미로 'if'를 사용할 때는 일이 벌어지는 시점의 시제를 사용 한다.

- The results will decide if he will work at a good company.

b. 'to-부정사'는 명사, 형용사, 부사적 쓰임새가 있는데, 이 문장에서는 '~할 정도로' 뜻을 지닌 부사적 용법으로 앞 절의 내용 전체를 수식하고 있는데, 형용사, 부사, 명사를 수식할 수도 있다.

- We don't have enough water to share.
- They have worked quickly enough to be praised.

영어 매체에서 한국 음식의 소개

◇ 각 음식별로 어떤 설명이 가장 적절하다고 생각하는지 설명 옆의 빈 칸에 1, 2위를 표시해봅시다.

Food	Media	Description	
bulgogi	Smithsonian	thinly sliced marinated beef	
	Hull Daily Mail	Korean beef brisket	
	www.longisland.com	marinated sliced rib eye	
	Washington Post	soy-marinated beef	
	Atlanta Journal Constitution	grilled marinated beef	
bibimbap	www.today.com	mixed vegetable and rice bowl with beef	
	Chesterfield Observer	an assortment of seasonal vegetables and beef over rice, topped with a fried egg and a spicy sauce	
	www.nj.com	rice mixed with assorted meats and vegetables	
	Los Angeles Times	mixed rice	
	NBC News	rice topped with vegetable, meat and sauce	
tteokbokki	Bon Appetit	spicy stir-fried rice cake	
	San Diego Union-Tribune	spicy rice cake	
	South China Morning Post	simmered rice cake	
	Atlanta Journal Constitution	stir-fried rice cake	
	San Francisco Chronicle	rice cake	
kimbap	Eater LA	rice and seaweed roll	
	New York Times	seaweed rice	
	Grand Rapids Business Journal	Korean-style fish and vegetable hand rolls wrapped with seaweed	
	www.chowhound.com	dried-seaweed-wrapped roll	
	• Los Angeles Times • Daily Breeze	Korean sushi roll	

How about your description?

bulgogi	
bibimbap	
tteokbokki	
kimbap	

Brookland's New Korean Fast-Casual Spot Serves Bibimbap Bowls Built for Delivery

Joon Park used to **cringe** when he would get takeout orders for his family's Korean barbecue restaurant in Annandale. "A lot of very traditional Korean dishes don't travel well," he says. "We couldn't figure it out how to deliver it to them. You get very **soggy** food in some styrofoam container." That's not the case at the Park family's new venture, Bangbop in Brookland. Orders like rainbow bibimbap bowls from the delivery and pickup-only shop at Tastemakers incubator/food hall are specifically designed **to still taste good** 30 minutes after traveling to diners in an eco-friendly container. The lengthy menu includes six different bibimbap bowls, along with spicy pork tacos, bulgogi **bao**, salads, Korean-inspired **bahn mi**, oven-fried organic Korean chicken wings, salads, build-your-own options, and more dishes.

source: www.dceater.com

* cringe: 움츠리다, (당황/혐오감 때문에) 움찔하다(=wince)
* soggy: 눅눅한
* to still taste good: 부사인 still을 'to+부정사' 사이에 사용한 표현으로 '여전히 맛이 좋다'
* bao: 만두를 뜻하는 중국어
* bahn mi: 빵을 뜻하는 베트남어

The **ghost kitchen** concept, which opened Monday, November 2, has been **in the works** even before the pandemic. "We've actually been planning or thinking about a delivery kitchen for a few years as our second act. We've done the traditional sit-down dining, traditional Korean restaurant thing," Park explains (the family opened its Annandale restaurant in 1998 and sold it over a decade ago). "We wanted to do something that's different and challenging—and something that actually kind of **marries** our family's tradition and expertise handed down from generations of Korean recipes, authentic flavors, and modernizing it with sort of a new business model," he says. Park's sister Ji is Bangbop's executive chef and manages the restaurant, while Joon is a **self-professed** technology **geek** who's into analyzing data and solving **logistics** problems.

spicy pork kimbap

spicy pork. pickled radish, carrots, spinach, egg, red cabbage, braised burdock. sesame oil, sesame seeds. side of spicy...

source: www.bangbop.com

* in the works: 진행 중인, 계획 중인. cf. 이 뜻인 경우 복수 명사 works를 사용해야 함
* marry: 연결하다, 통합하다(=combine, blend)
* self-professed: 스스로 인정하는(=acknowledged by oneself)
* geek: 특정한 분야(특히, 컴퓨터)에 뛰어난 지식을 가진 사람
* logistics: 물류

"Focus on Terminology"

◆ ghost kitchen

ghost kitchen은 2015년 *NBC New York*의 기사에서 처음 사용된 용어로 매장 내나 밖에 의자가 없는 주로 배달 만을 전문으로 하는 식당을 가리키는데 배달 음식에 대한 수요만큼이나 급속히 성장하고 있는 사업 모델이다. 일부 가게는 take-out이나 drive-through 서비스를 하는 경우도 있다. 기존 식당의 kitchen과 또 다른 차이점은 하나의 식당 브랜드만이 아니라 여러 브랜드들의 음식을 제공하기도 한다. delivery-only restaurant, virtual kitchen, shadow kitchen, commissary kitchen, cloud kitchen 또는 dark kitchen이라고도 한다.

"I really think of ghost or dark kitchens as almost an e-commerce technology business as much as it is a restaurant," he says. Besides a **slick** website, Bangbop incorporates technology that automates dispatches of drivers, using three different outside companies to make sure the restaurant can handle peak times. The restaurant offers deliveries within three miles of its site in Brookland (other food delivery platforms will take deliveries further out, up to five or six miles or so).

* slick: 영리하게 잘 만든(=adroitly devised)

"Focus on Grammar"

◈ as much as

"I really think of ghost or dark kitchens as almost an e-commerce technology business as much as it is a restaurant," he says.

'A as much as B'는 'B 만큼 A 하다' 뜻을 지닌 'as ~ as' 구문을 활용한 동급비교의 대표적 표현이다. 위 문장은 'ghost kitchens를 하나의 식당으로 여기는 만큼 e-commerce 기술 사업으로도 생각한다' 의미이다. as ~ as 구문을 활용한 동급 비교 표현으로 as long as, as far as, as well as, as many ~ as, as little ~ as 등을 들 수 있다. 이들 표현의 부정문은 not as/so ~ as를 사용한다.

- They are soap opera addicts and watch as much as they can.
- You can call me at work as long as you don't make a habit of it.
- The best companies are those that are fully responsible for their products as far as they can.
- She is an individual as well as being the general manager's wife.
- Janet already knows as many words in German as she does in Dutch.
- It takes as little as one second to lose attention and cause an accident.
- There are not as many stores as there were.
- I realize that one's mental processes in old age are not so sharp as they once were.

Besides focusing on takeout, the Parks wanted to put a healthful, sustainably-sourced **spin** on Korean barbecue—one that appeals to people with dietary restrictions. "With every menu item, we thought about how to make it healthier, without compromising taste," Park says. "Our customers really love the fact that we offer vegan and non-meat options like tofu." There's also "Impossible Bulgogi," made with **Impossible Foods** vegan protein. So far, Bangbop's most popular dish is the traditional bulgogi bibimbap, which Park says tastes as "if you had a Korean grandmother who cooked really well and she made a bowl of bibimbap for you the best way she knows how."

Park says that customers in Brookland have embraced the restaurant so far, and he hopes to pay it forward by hiring employees from the local community as the restaurant grows. A **PoPville** post led to even more orders than the family expected in its first few weeks of business. "Since late last week, we've really been working really, really hard to make sure we are delivering great food and we're running out of ingredients," he says.

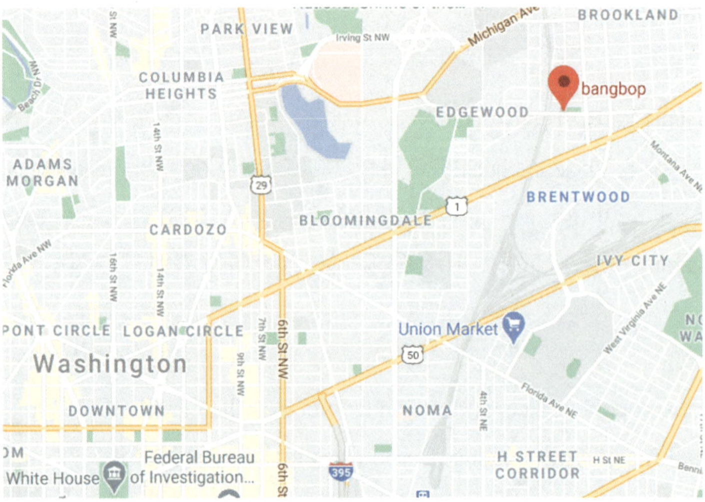

source: www.google.com/maps

* spin: 독특한 특징
* Impossible Foods: 식물(plant-based) 재료로 만든 고기나 생선을 판매하는 회사
* PoPville: Washington, DC 지역 디지털 언론 매체

◇ 어떤 K-food에 대한 설명인지 맞혀봅시다.

a. ____________ is a staple Korean dish that requires little culinary skills, where chunky slices of pork belly are cooked on a grill at the diners' table. It's then wrapped in lettuce or sesame leaf with dipping sauces and accompaniments such as mushrooms, green chili peppers, raw onions and garlic, as well as kimchi.

b. ____________ uses thick handmade wheat noodles topped with raw cucumber slices and a mixture of salty black soybean paste, diced pork and vegetables. Priced from 5,000 won onwards, this hearty noodle dish is great for when you need a quick meal that doesn't break the wallet.

c. ____________ is usually served in a stainless steel bowl with a cold broth, shredded cucumbers, Korean pear slices, boiled egg, and slices of cold boiled beef. The long and thin noodles are made from flour or buckwheat. Symbolizing longevity of life and good health, the noodles are traditionally served without cutting, but diners can request for waiters to cut the noodles according to their preference.

d. ____________ consists of a small spring chicken stuffed with chestnuts, garlic, dried jujubes, ginseng, glutinous rice, and gingko nuts. The ingredients are then slow-cooked until the meat is very tender and the thick broth permeates a slightly bitter yet fragrant taste.

e. ____________ is a traditional Korean noodle dish made up of stir-fried sweet potato, thinly shredded vegetables, beef, and a hint of soy sauce and sugar. Depending on the chef, additional ingredients like mushrooms are added to the mix. It is known for its sweet and flavorful taste and its soft yet slightly chewy texture.

f. ____________ is a hot soup made from ox bones, ox meat and briskets, often seasoned with salt, ground black pepper, chopped green onions, or minced garlic according to the consumer's taste. The broth is of a milky white, cloudy color and is often eaten with rice.

g. ____________ is a unique dish made of pig's intestines stuffed with several ingredients such as noodles, pork blood, and sweet rice. Its versions differ in fillings and wrappings, and are often prepared differently according to the province in Korea.

London에 있는 Korean restaurants 방문객들의 후기

☺ Tteokbokki and kalbi were delicious! Visited Korean restaurant for the first time and it now becomes one of my favorite restaurants for sure.

☺ The food is so delicious and the staff are actually really nice! I LOVE the bibimbap. The only con is that the place is so, so tiny so we go at like 11 in the morning but it's worth the travelling and I love Tottenham Court road so it is always a treat coming here.

☺ The menu has all the basics from jeons to kimbaps, bibimbap, meat sets, stews, and soups. We had the kimchi jeon (best we've had in London), veggie kimbap, tteokbokki with dumplings, Korean miso soup, and a side of rice. Everything was incredibly delicious and soooo cheap (total was under £25 for 2). There are only 15 seats so come 10 minutes before opening or be prepared to wait. Downstairs is more kpop graffiti and a small store.

☺ Amazing food with friendly staffs. We have ordered Bibimbab, Gamja Tang, KFC chicken, Seafood Pancake. It sounds a lot but we had them all. These food are the one you must try, unfortunately we didn't have more space for Jajang Myeon and Jjam Bong but for sure we will be back for them soon. Can't wait!!

☺ Refreshingly authentic Korean in the heart of London. Highly recommend the BBQ sets, and the Korean Fried Chicken. Come here hungry, as you'll want to try everything!

☹ It is ok, but I'm not convinced. Had a bibimbap takeaway and I wasn't satisfied with the portion. You could put more rice, the bowl is big enough. Good service though; I will occasionally return for lunches as I work in the area. Hope the portions will be something they will look at and improve.

☹ This was a pretty disappointing experience. Firstly, there is no kimchi/free starters as in all Korean restaurants. You just sit there, waiting. Secondly, the food takes forever to arrive. Thirdly, the food is bland—we ordered a seafood pancake which was pure flour mixed with a spring onion, no seafood whatsoever. Our mandoo soup had broken dumplings and tasteless soup/broth, and a simple chicken dish was outrageously oily. For the price, this was unacceptable. Will skip.

☹ Ordered bibimbap, arrived after literally 1 min after ordering, barely warm in a cold metal bowl topped with a cold fried egg. Definitely the worst bibimbap I've ever had. Why would you serve something usually served in a hot stone dish in a cold metal bucket?

☹ The chicken was ok but that was it, the salad we ordered was just shaved veggie raw with bowl of rice underneath with no dressing, I can't stress enough, it was with no dressing, tasteless and I can't even believe chef showed it to be on the menu, even if this is authentic, as an establishment they have to select a good that's worth the money people are paying for. The kimchi jjigae was like a soup, there was barely 2 tbsp of kimchi cabbage in it with 2 slim shaves of pork, not worth the money, rice comes separate, the rest of the starters were the same absolutely no taste, believe me if you want to enjoy food this is not the restaurant to go. By the way we paid £30 per person so it's not on the cheap side either.

☹ Food was disgusting especially the bulgogi bbq, andddddd it's too pricy for this quality of food.

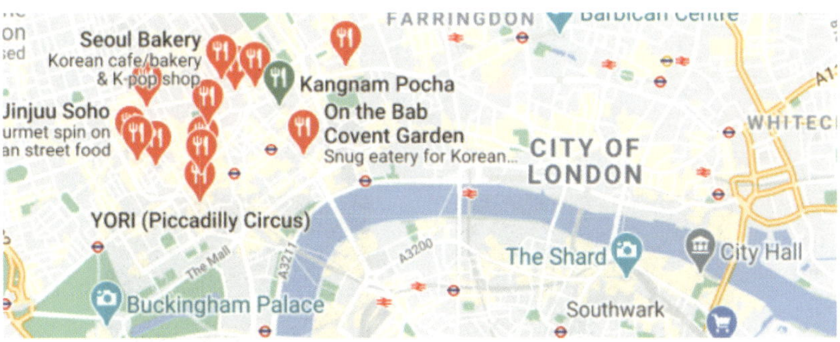

source: www.google.com/maps

Write your own reviews.

최근에 먹었던 음식 중에서 맛있었던 음식 두 가지와 별로였던 음식 두 가지에 대한 후기를 영어로 작성해봅시다.

★★★★★

★★★★☆

★★☆☆☆

★☆☆☆☆

Get Croiffles (a Croissant-Waffle Hybrid) and Dalgona Coffees at Seoul Sweetie, a New Korean Dessert Bar in Adelaide's CBD

The team behind late-night Korean diner Busan Baby have opened a new venue next door. Enter for croiffles, bubble-tea ice-cream, bingsu and that other 2020 viral sensation—whipped instant coffee. We've had cronuts and cruffins. Now the croiffle—yes, that's a **cross** between a croissant and a waffle—has arrived in Adelaide. The pastry hybrid is one of the stars at Seoul Sweetie, a new Korean dessert bar from the crew behind Busan Baby (and located right next door).

Co-owner and head chef Jinny Shim, who's behind the popular chiffon cakes at Busan Baby and Bai Long Store, says she's been looking for somewhere to present her desserts as the main attraction. "I used to work in restaurants as a pastry chef, but the desserts were just a small section of the whole menu," Shim tells *Broadsheet*. "I always wanted to do my own thing with more creativity, flavours and seasonal fruit."

With a background as a painter and a furniture designer, Shim says she has an artistic approach to constructing her desserts. "I always think my dishes are like a canvas—the colours, textures and flavours have to go together," she says. "I really like to mix Western and Asian flavours and surprise people with the combinations."

* cross: 혼종(=hybrid)

"Focus on Terminology"

◆ hybrid food

chizza	chicken + pizza	mushronnara	mushroom + carbonara
cronut	croissant + doughnut	sushirrito	sushi + burrito
cragel	croissant + bagel	paffle	pumpkin pie + waffle
lotzel	lobster tail + pretzel	tacro	taco + croissant

Take the aforementioned croiffles, which are served with either **matcha** ice-cream, whipped white-chocolate **ganache** or chocolate mousse. Or the strawberry **panna cotta** served with strawberry-**umeshu** sorbet, chiffon cake, raspberry **meringue**, whipped cream cheese and white-chocolate ganache.

There are also two kinds of bingsu (a popular Korean shaved-ice dessert): mango with lychee popping pearls and mango-coconut jelly, and bubble-tea ice-cream with Oreo crumbs and boba pearls.

Shim's rendition of dalgona coffee, a whipped instant-coffee drink that went viral earlier this year, is the product of countless hours of experimentation. It's made with Starbucks instant coffee and topped with honeycomb, and available in three flavours (including mocha and matcha). The team's also pouring T2 teas and Vittoria coffee.

* matcha: 녹차가루
* ganache: 초콜릿과 크림을 섞은 것
* panna cotta: 크림, 설탕, 우유를 젤라틴과 섞어 만드는 이태리 디저트
* umeshu: 매실주. ume=일본어로 매실
* meringue: 머랭(달걀 흰자와 설탕을 섞은 것)

panna cotta

lychee

boba pearls

Vittoria coffee

While Seoul Sweetie is separate **entity** from Busan Baby, Shim says the new venue is a "natural progression". Together, the two venues provide a glimpse into South Korea's **vibrant**, late-night food and drink scene. The **earthy fit-out** was designed by Shim, who took inspiration from the novel *Norwegian Wood* by Japanese author Haruki Murakami. The result feels like a cosy woodland **retreat**, with **ambient** light fittings hanging from wooden branches, greenery, and Shim's own interpretation of *The Arrival of Spring*, a painting by English artist David Hockney.

source: Seoul Sweetie's facebook

* entity: 사업체, 조직
* vibrant: 생기 넘치는, 활기찬(=energetic, dynamic, vigorous)
* earthy: 정제되지 않은(=unrefined), 투박한(=coarse, crude)
* fit-out: 장식
* retreat: 편안한 공간(=a place affording peace, quiet, privacy, or security)
* ambient: 잔잔한(=creating a relaxing atmosphere)

The Arrival of Spring by David Hockney. source: www.royalacademy.org.uk

How to get to sleep: Take this herbal extract every day to improve sleep quality

One in three people in the UK suffer from sleep deprivation and the causes are numerous and often interacting. Working into the early hours at a computer screen can make it hard to switch off, for example. While it is important to address unhealthy lifestyle habits, it may not be possible to implement **sweeping** changes. Fortunately, you do not have to. Evidence shows that simple dietary **tweaks** can reset your body clock.

source: www.clevelandclinic.org

* sweeping: 광범위한(=wide-ranging, comprehensive), 완전한(=complete)
* tweak: 수정, 조정(=modification, adjustment)

Focus on Grammar

◈ 가목적어 'it'

One in three people in the UK suffer from sleep deprivation and the causes are numerous and often interacting. Working into the early hours at a computer screen can make *it* hard to switch off, for example.

'it'의 쓰임새는 광범위하다. 앞에 쓰인 명사를 지칭하거나, 앞 문장 전체를 지칭하는 경우도 있다. 위 문장의 경우 'it'은 가목적어 그리고 'to switch off'는 진목적어 역할을 한다. 수면 부족의 원인이 다양하며 서로 상관관계를 가지고 있는데, 예를 들어, 새벽에(또는 아침 일찍) 컴퓨터 작업을 하므로 전등을 끄는(하는 일을 중단하는)게 어려울 수도 있다(즉, 업무상/lifestyle 때문에 수면 부족을 겪는다)를 뜻한다.

There are a range of dietary items that have been shown to improve sleep quality. One that has yielded promising results is red ginseng extract, which is derived from the Korean red ginseng plant that grows in Asia. In a recent study published in the Journal of **Ethnopharmacology**, 15 healthy male participants 15-37 years-old were given 1,500 milligrams of red ginseng by mouth three times daily for seven days to assess the potential effects of ginseng on sleep quality. Sleep quality was evaluated through overnight polysomnography (a test used to diagnose sleep disorders) given one day before and seven days after ginseng supplementation was administered. Various outcome measures, including sleep **efficacy**, total sleep time, proportion of sleep stages and wakefulness after falling asleep, were evaluated. The researchers found that sleep efficacy was significantly increased and total wake time was significantly reduced following ginseng supplementation. Rapid Eye Movement (REM) sleep also significantly increased.

source: www.express.co.uk

* ethnopharmacology: 민족 약학(특정 민족들의 민간요법에 대한 과학적인 연구)
* efficacy: 효율(=effectiveness)

Focus on Grammar

◈ 관계대명사와 **'be'** 동사의 생략

15 healthy male participants 15-37 years-old were given 1,500 milligrams of red ginseng ...

주격관계대명사와 'be'동사는 시제와 상관없이 생략할 수 있는데, 위 문장의 경우 '15 healthy male participants who/that were 15-37 years-old'에서 'who/that were'를 생략하고 있다.

According to the National Sleep Foundation (NSF), REM sleep is the final phase of sleep where your brain becomes more active. "REM sleep plays an important role in learning and memory function, since this is when your brain **consolidates** and processes information from the day before so that it can be stored in your long-term memory," explains the health body. It is not exactly clear how ginseng has a sleep-inducing effect but it may be partly linked to its ability to **alleviate** anxiety, which can cause sleep problems.

According to a review published in the Journal of Ginseng Research (JGR), ginseng **suppresses** "the occurrence of psychological diseases such as anxiety and depression".

* consolidate: 강화하다(=strengthen, solidify)
* alleviate: 완화하다(=reduce, ease)
* suppress: 억제하다(=subdue)

◇ Red ginseng의 수면 문제 개선효과를 홍보하는 영어 광고 문구를 작성해봅시다.

< Famous Chef Quotes About Food >

- I maintain standards and I strive for perfection. That level of pressure is conveyed in a very bullish way and that's what cooking is all about. — Gordon Ramsay

- A recipe has no soul. You, as the cook, must bring soul to the recipe. — Thomas Keller

- If an architect makes a mistake, he grows ivy to cover it. If a doctor makes a mistake, he covers it with soil. If a cook makes a mistake, he covers it with some sauce and says it is a new recipe. — Paul Bocuse

- A cook is creative, marrying ingredients in the way a poet marries words. — Roger Verge

- Remember that a very good sardine is always preferable to a not that good lobster. — Ferran Adria

- Chefs have a new opportunity—and perhaps even an obligation—to inform the public about what is good to eat, and why. — Rene Redzepi

- The most powerful social media... it is not the internet, it is not Facebook—it is food. This connects all human beings. — Alex Atala

- After my long period working in five star hotel and Michelin style restaurant, I really enjoy working as a private chef more because you get to see your work being enjoyed giving you that first hand feeling to do more for the host and guest. — Darius Williams

- Tasting a dish should be memorable. If nothing remains in the memory of a single guest, then I have made a mistake. — Alain Ducasse

- Food is one of life's greatest joys yet we've reached this really sad point where we're turning food into the enemy, and something to be afraid of. — Jamie Oliver

- After years of working in professional kitchens, and then spending so much time in a lot of different home kitchens, I realized that there's a huge gap in the market where you have people who develop cookware but who don't actually cook. — Curtis Stone

- I always tell people a clean cooking area is a clean mind which is available for the creativity. — Carla Hall

Cross-word Puzzle

ACROSS

2. a small quantity
4. crude in style
6. to behave in a timid way
10. free of debt
12. showing a willingness to take risks
13. one who knows a lot about a certain subject
14. to grow vigorously
15. of prime importance

DOWN

1. a first attempt
3. showing extreme care
5. to be strongly attracted
7. one who has an enthusiastic interest in food
8. skillfully performed
9. the sense of taste
11. having a pleasantly sharp flavor
15. unpleasantly wet and soft

Chapter V

K-BEAUTY

The 12 Korean Beauty Trends to Try in 2021, According to the Experts

Snail **mucin**. Bee **venom**. Glass skin. These are just some of the beauty trends to emerge from South Korea in the past five years. Whether you've **dabbled** in a bit of donkey milk (good for rejuvenating the skin with protein and fatty acids) or you've played it safe with a weekly face mask, K-beauty is everywhere. In fact, Allied Market Research says that by 2026, the K-beauty market will be worth an estimated $21 billion. According to Jenni Middleton, director of beauty at trend forecasting company WGSN, "During the coronavirus pandemic, consumers searched more for K-beauty, looking for innovative products to add to their **lockdown beauty regimes**."

Like most cultural phenomena, K-beauty is ever-changing—what was big last year may not be as popular this year. As Middleton observes, we're seeing the traditional 10-step routine give way to a more minimalist approach as conscious consumers react against fast fashion and excessive packaging. Elsewhere, playful gimmicks such as color-changing effects or jellylike substances are being passed over in favor of science-backed formulas.

* mucin: 진액
* venom: (뱀, 거미, 전갈, 벌 등의) 독
* dabble: 담그다, 적시다 > 당나귀 우유로 만든 body wash 제품을 사용할 때의 동작
* lockdown beauty regime: (pandemic으로 인해 마스크를 착용해야 하므로 자유롭게 화장을 할 수 없는 상황에서) 통제된(제한적인) 화장법

source: www.skinkraft.com

To find out more about the biggest K-beauty trends of 2021, we spoke to some of the industry's leading skin-care experts.

Charlotte Cho, founder of Soko Glam

1. Hanbang ingredients
"Hanbang ingredients are traditional herbal ingredients used in Korean medicines and they've long been a staple in Korean life. For example, ginseng root, **houttuynia cordata**, **sacred lotus**, and **rehmannia** boast antiaging, **anti-inflammation**, and **regenerative** properties."

2. Acid layering
"K-beauty has been incorporating more acid into its products, but with a gentle approach that focuses on striking the balance: Too much can irritate and aggravate your skin, too little will yield no results, so products with an optimal amount is key. Use the right balance of AHAs and BHAs (plant and animal-derived acids) to gently **exfoliate** dead skin cells and smooth skin texture."

3. Carrot seed oil
"Carrot seed oil is an unsung hero at the moment, although it has been used in K-beauty for more than 10 years. It contains vitamin A and is a great antioxidant. It's antiaging, **antifungal**, antibacterial, and anti-inflammatory—so it's ideal for anyone looking to brighten up their skin."

* houttuynia cordata: 어성초
* sacred lotus: 연꽃
* rehmannia: (약용식물) 지황
* anti-inflammation: 소염
* regenerative: 재생시키는(=reviving, restorative)
* exfoliate: 벗겨내다
* antifungal: 항곰팡이의, 항균의

Houttuynia cordata
source: www.nparks.gov.sg

4. Gentle retinol

"K-beauty's 'skin first' approach will continue through 2021, especially given that self-care and skin care are so important right now. There's no denying retinol's powerful antiaging properties, but the K-beauty approach uses a lower percentage, so the skin stays healthier and less irritated. Retinol is highly efficacious without causing unnecessary damage."

Coco Park, founder of The Beauty Wolf and coauthor of *Korean Beauty Secrets*

5. Centella asiatica

"[The year] 2021 is less about what's '**buzzy**' and more about what's tried-and-true, with a focus on calming the skin. Centella asiatica [an herb grown in Asia, known for being anti-inflammatory]—or 'cica'—is huge right now. With everyone dealing with the prolonged stress of the pandemic and dreaded '**maskne**,' soothing irritated, angry skin seems to be at the forefront of people's minds. Cica is the ingredient that everyone wants to add to their routine."

* buzzy: 흥미로운(=eye-catching), 고대하는(=anticipating)

Focus on Terminology

◈ maskne=mask + acne

Covid-19 시기에 생긴 신조어로, 매일 같이 mask를 쓰고 다녀 생긴 여드름

◈ Covid-19가 만들어낸 신조어

- covidiot: 사회적 거리두기(social distancing)를 지키지 않는 사람
- covedio party: Zoom이나 Skype같은 화상 프로그램을 이용한 온라인 파티
- quranteams: 봉쇄 조치로 인해 온라인상에 만든 팀
- WFH: working from home
- spendemic: pandemic으로 인한 온라인 쇼핑의 증가 현상
- quaranbaking: 봉쇄 시기에 빵을 구우면서 위안을 찾는 것

Elisa Lee, founder of Dot Dot Skin

6. Clean beauty

"More brands are developing products free of chemical additives, artificial ingredients, and fragrance. Products will be even more gentle with effective plant-based ingredients, and many brands are becoming vegan as well. Consumers are more aware of what they put on their skin."

Sarah Oh, founder of Oh My Gloss!

7. Pre-, pro-, and postbiotics

"This year, inner and outer wellness brands and products will gain more popularity. For example, brands that focus on pre-, pro-, and postbiotics; **microbiome**-friendly skin care; and consumable supplements, which benefit both the skin and the gut.

K-beauty will shift more towards a holistic approach, linking skin care and internal health. I take probiotic supplements for my **bouts** of **eczema** and I love using K-beauty products with fermented ingredients. I regularly use 107—it uses aged [seven- and 10-year-old] vinegar [that promotes good gut health]. Their vinegar tastes delicious with honey!"

source: www.107beauty.com

* microbiome: 미생물군
* bout: 싸움, 병치레(=a period of illness)

Focus on Terminology

◈ 화장품 사용으로 생기는 피부 트러블

blister	수포	hives	두드러기
burning	작열감	inflammation	염증
comedone formation	모공 폐쇄	pigmentation	색소침착
contact dermatitis	접촉성 피부염	red rash	붉은 발진(뾰루지)
eczema	습진	rosacea	빨간코

Jude Chao, founder of Fifty Shades of Snail and author of *Skin Care for Your Soul*

8. Flexible minimalism

"A few years back, we were **oversaturated** with the '10-step Korean skin-care routine.' The 'skin-care diet' [using fewer products and steps] that followed was a **pushback** against that, but it was too restrictive for those who wanted more results than could be attained with just the basics.

Flexible minimalism is a focus on clean and simple product lines, which makes customizing your routine easier. There will also be a push towards **pared-back** lists of ingredients. Single and minimal ingredients are appealing because of their simplicity and high concentration of the hero component."

* oversaturated: 과포화된(=excessively charged)
* pushback: 반발, 저항(=resistance as to a policy)
* pared-back: 축소된

"Focus on Grammar"

◆ than이하에서 생략

... it was too restrictive for those who wanted more results *than could be attained with just the basics*.

이 문장은 비교급 구문에서 흔히 볼 수 있는 than이하에서 앞 절과 공통분모를 생략하는 경우(주어와 동사의 생략, 또는 동사와 목적어의 생략)와는 차이가 있는 매우 예외적인 생략의 방식을 택하고 있다.

문맥상으로 이 문장은 '기초 제품만으로 얻을 수 있는 결과 보다 더 많은 결과를 원하는 소비자들에게 skin-care diet는 너무 제한적이었다'를 의미한다. 따라서 생략된 요소를 포함하면 'more results than the results which could be attained with just the basics' 같은 구문이 된다.

Alicia Yoon, founder of Peach & Lily

9. At-home indulgences
"Skin care has a functional element—it has to work and deliver results—but I expect products that provide meditative, soothing, and spa-like moments to take off in a big way. They can transport you mentally and emotionally to another **headspace**."

Sarah Lee and *Christine Chang*, cofounders of Glow Recipe

10. **Hyphenate** and hybrid skin care
"We've started seeing 'skipcare' as a K-beauty trend, where the focus is on a pared-down, simple, and minimalist routine. We will be seeing more efficient and effective multitasking and versatile products—what we like to call 'hyphenates' or 'hybrid' skin care."

11. Skin **detoxifying** and barrier strengthening
"The belief that 'skin is a reflection of your mental state' comes from Korea, and growing up, my mother emphasized this to me many times. We'll see more barrier-strengthening ingredients that boost immunity, such as mushrooms, plus detoxifying herbs including **mugwort** and ginger. Ceramides [which form a protective layer to help prevent moisture loss and visible skin damage] will make a comeback too."

source: www.amazon.com

* headspace: 정신상태(=a person's state of mind or mindset)
* hyphenate: 여러 가지 역할을 하는 사람/물건
* detoxify: 독성을 없애다
* mugwort: 쑥

◇ 다음 단어와 같은 의미를 지닌 단어를 위 글에서 찾아봅시다.

1. wall	2. procedure	3. resistance
4. manifestation	5. carry (v.)	6. emollient

12. A boost in body care
"In Korea, many body-care rituals originate from the bathhouse culture, where milk treatments are **slathered** on the face and body, and baths are **steeped** with skin-beneficial ingredients, such as green tea and probiotics. During a difficult year, personal self-care has taken on new importance for many, so we expect to see the definition to include all of the skin, from head to toe."

* slather: 듬뿍 바르다(=spread in large amounts)
* steep: 담그다(=immerse, soak), 깊이 스며들게 하다

<한국 화장품 브랜드의 영어 광고 슬로건>

Brand	Advertising Slogan
banila co.	Contemporary Beautyware
belif	believe in truth
Donginbi	DISCOVER THE BEAUTY OF GINSENG
Dr.Jart+	skincare powered by science, inspired by art
ETUDE House	Wannabe Sweet? PLAY ETUDE
HANSKIN	Natural Science
innisfree	The pure island where clean nature and healthy beauty coexist in harmony
It's Skin	Clinical Skin Solution
LANEIGE	• Unleash the Sparkling beauty in you! • The true hydration experts
MISSHA	LOVE YOUR SKIN, LOVE YOUR SOUL
NATURE REPUBLIC	journey to nature
Skin Food	cosmetics made with exquisitely delicious food
SNP	Shining Nature Purity
Sulwhasoo	Holistic beauty from Asian wisdom
THE**FACE**SHOP	NATURAL STORY
The History of Whoo	The One and Only Precious, The History of Whoo.
the SAEM	inspired by global ecology
Tony Moly	WITTY BEAUTY
WELCOS	more than beauty

외국인의 한국 화장품 사용 후기

skincare	☺ I have very sensitive skin and it's rare that I find products that I can use every day. Korean skincare items seem to be the exception for me. ☺ Closes up pores and gives your skin a smooth texture ☺ I love this hydrating toner. It's moisturizing. I had issues with severe dryness on my forehead, area around my nose and chin. After one use, I immediately saw instant results. A little bit goes a long way. It's very light weight. It does not feel heavy or thick. ☺ I LOVE this serum! It's so refreshing to put on my face and the color is beautiful! I would definitely purchase again!
face moisturizer	☺ I ♥ this product. I like the smell when I first open the lid. I tried both the serum and the cream moisturizer. I applied the product at night, I wake up with soft, moist, and hydrated skin. I do feel that product absorbs into my skin. Let me just say that this product owns up to every word it says. ☺ I've been using this product for over a year now, and it's easily my all-time favorite moisturizer. I have extremely sensitive skin and this doesn't give me any redness or breakouts. It doesn't leave any greasy residue.
foundation makeup	☺ I really like this cushion product. It feels very light; yet you can build up the color. It does offer a light to medium coverage. Feels like you're wearing nothing at all and doesn't wipe off on your collar or the phone! ☺ This is the third time I've ordered this cushion, and it never disappoints. It has buildable, medium coverage and has 50 SPF! It tends to come off the oily areas of my face after a few hours but I don't mind because application is so easy, I just reapply in any restroom.
eye makeup	☺ I have heard that Korean eyeshadow isn't very pigmented, but I found this to be just right. You can use the lighter shades for a wash of color if you want, and the darker bolder shades give more of a punch.

	☺ The shadows are so buttery and soft, and the colors are perfect for everyday wear! If you're a fan of soft, Korean-style makeup then this is a must have. The glitters are so beautiful!
facial mask	☺ I had heard a lot about this mask but wasn't able to purchase it in the US until now. It is great! The material is super soft (they use cotton for their masks) and I noticed a difference in my skin immediately after use. ☺ These masks are the perfect addition to my 7 step Korean skincare routine. My skin is ridiculously sensitive so anything even remotely fragranced breaks me out but these masks really brighten my skin and cools my redness down after double cleansing, especially since I keep them in the fridge for 10 minutes before application. My skin has never looked better. Great product.

Write your own reviews.

여러분이 사용하고 있는 화장품에 대한 후기를 영어로 써봅시다.

★★★★★

____

____

____

★★☆☆☆

____

____

____

K-beauty comes to Turkey as Korean cosmetics exports boom

After K-pop and K-drama, the latest Korean export surging in popularity in Turkey and the Middle East is K-beauty. According to data from Turkey's largest e-commerce company, Trendyol, sales of South Korean cosmetics on its platform have been running five times higher than a year ago. The figures suggest the South Korean beauty industry is opening up another new export market, as its sales rise across the globe.

Last year was "a milestone year" for the category, a representative of the e-commerce platform said, and sales have continued to soar in 2021. After selling 665,000 South Korean cosmetics items on the platform in 2020—up from 135,000 in 2019—that figure had already been surpassed by April this year. The number of items sold in the first half was five times higher than the same period last year, the representative said. Trendyol began selling K-beauty products only in 2018.

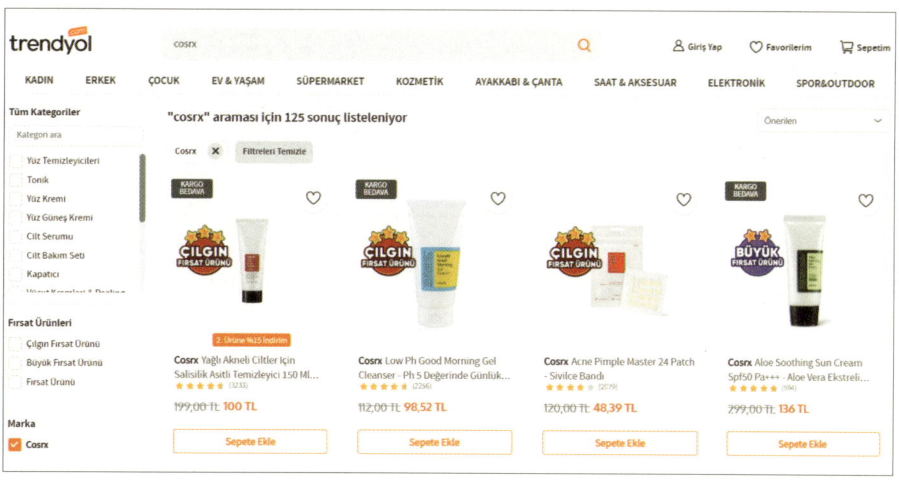

source: www.trendyol.com

South Korean brands such as Cosrx, Missha, Klairs and Axis-Y have gained a **foothold** in Turkey thanks to the e-commerce boom and social media influencers, mostly selling via local distributors.

* foothold: 기반(=a secure position/basis)

"I kept hearing, 'I watched this Korean music band video and watched that Korean drama where everyone has skin as smooth as glass, where women do not age. How come?'" said Cisem Cakir, an influencer with nearly 200,000 YouTube subscribers and more than 16 million views on her account "Naturally **Serein**." Cakir works with brands such as Cosrx, Missha and Moremo. She argued that Korean brands have a value-for-money edge over U.S. and European brands.

South Korea's cosmetics exports to the Middle East reached $7.8 million in June, up from $7.0 million in the same month last year and $4.3 million in June 2019, according to the country's trade ministry. Foundation and other types of makeup accounted for the largest share, followed by face wash products, the ministry said.

South Korea exported $726 million of cosmetics globally in June, meaning the Middle East remains a relatively small market. China is the biggest destination for K-beauty exports, followed by the U.S. and Japan, and demand has been booming around the world.

Global K-beauty product sales are forecast to reach $13.9 billion by 2027, according to India-based Allied Market Research, up from $10.2 billion in 2019.

* serein: (특히 열대지방에서) 일몰 후 맑은 하늘에서 내리는 가는 비

◇ 다음 정의에 해당하는 단어를 위 글에서 찾아봅시다.

1. A slight competitive advantage or superiority: ____________
2. To prosper rapidly: ____________
3. The place to which a person or thing travels or is sent: ____________
4. To become old or show signs of becoming old: ____________
5. One of the parts into which something has been divided: ____________
6. A private access to a computer system or online service, usually requiring a password to enter: ____________
7. A group of musicians who play modern music together: ____________

Trendyol, in which Chinese e-commerce giant Alibaba owns a majority stake, accounts for about a third of Turkey's e-commerce market. This month it became the country's first "**decacorn**"—a startup worth over $10 billion—after a fundraising round by investors including SoftBank Group's Vision Fund 2 and General Atlantic.

South Korean skin care products now have a market share of 8% on the platform, Trendyol said, up 3 percentage points in the past year, and some categories are growing even faster. South Korean makeup brands have jumped from a 3% market share last year to 8% so far this year.

The growth stems from higher demand, new product launches and wider distribution. The number of K-beauty brands available on Trendyol has reached 90, up from 66 two years ago, it said, while the number of merchants offering South Korean products has jumped to 150 from 22 over the same period.

And it is not only online where K-beauty is **making inroads** in Turkey. Watsons, the Hong Kong-based drugstore chain, has designated sections for 11 South Korean skin care brands at more than 300 of its almost 350 stores in Turkey, the company's local trade and marketing director told Nikkei. Beauty product chain Sephora is also promoting K-beauty in Turkey.

* make inroads: 진출하다

Focus on Terminology

◈ decacorn

decacorn은 벤처 자본가 Aileen Lee가 2013년 경제 용어로 처음 사용한 unicorn에서 파생한 용어이다. unicorn은 머리에 뿔이 하나 달린 상상속의 동물로, 기업 가치가 $1 billion 이상으로 평가 받는 비상장 신생 벤처기업을 지칭한다. decacorn은 머리에 뿔이 10개 달린 상상속의 동물로, 기업 가치가 $10 billion 이상으로 평가 받는 비상장 신생 벤처기업을 뜻하는 단어이다.

Apart from Turkey, Watsons announced in October of last year that it opened its first store in the Middle East in the United Arab Emirates and has plans to open 100 more in the region, including in Saudi Arabia, by the end of 2025. That is likely to provide a further boost for the spread of K-beauty products.

Korean cosmetics sold at Watsons in Turkey

source: www.watsons.com.tr

Startup business 관련 terminology

• Angel investor — 기술력은 있으나 창업을 위한 자금이 부족한 초기 단계의 startup company에 자금 지원과 경영 지도를 해주는 개인투자자를 말한다. 자금이 시급한 벤처기업에 갑작스럽게 나타나 돈을 출자해주기 때문에 angel이라는 이름이 붙었다. business angel 또는 angel funder라고도 한다.

• Bootstrapping — startup company가 외부의 자금 지원을 받지 않고 자체 조달 자금으로 기업 운영을 시작하는 것을 뜻한다. 부츠 신발 끈을 다른 사람의 도움을 받지 않고 스스로 묶는 것을 비유적으로 표현한 것이다.

• Burn rate — 기업의 현금 소진율을 말하는데 주로 월 단위로 표현한다. 차기 외부 투자를 받기 위한 시간을 측정하는데 활용한다.

• Disrupting — 기업이 제품이나 기술로 관련 산업에 혁신을 불러일으키는 것을 의미한다. disruptive innovation 같은 표현을 사용한다.

• Exit strategy — 기업의 창립자, 경영자가 자사의 가치를 높인 이후 회사를 매각, 양도, 합병, 청산하거나 기업 공개 등을 통해 자금을 회수하는 전략이다.

• Hockey stick — 기업이 서서히 성장하다가 어느 시점에 급격히 성장하는 패턴이 hockey stick과 비슷한 경우에 비유적 표현으로 사용한다.

• IPO (Initial Public Offering) — 비상장기업이 상장하기 위해 법적인 절차와 방법에 따라 주식을 불특정 다수의 투자자들에게 팔고 재무내용을 공시하는 것이다.

• NDA (Non Disclosure Agreement) — 기업의 비밀을 보호하기 위해 기밀 누설로 인한 피해에 대한 책임을 지도록 하는 법적 서류이다.

• Seed Round or Seed Stage — 창업 아이템을 개발하고 시제품을 생산하는데 필요한 자금 조달 단계이다. 이후 자금 조달 단계는 Series A, B, C, D, E 등으로 부른다.

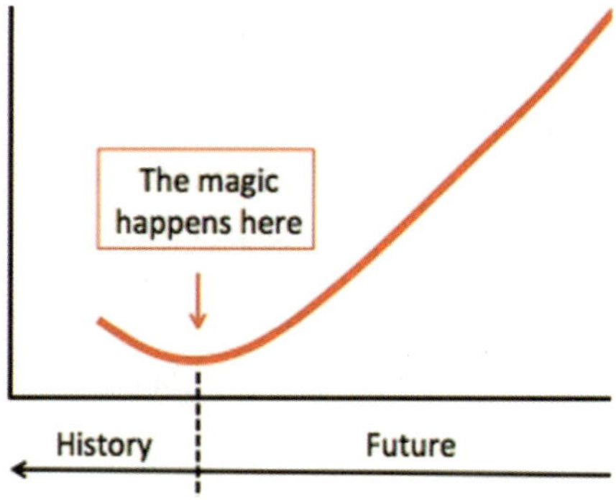

Hockey Stick Chart

source: www.corporatefinanceinstitute.com

K-Beauty regimes are ruling India, claims study data

While Bangalore and Delhi register the highest sales in metros, Guwahati and Lucknow drive maximum sales from the **tier** 2 market. Face care has become the most popular category (80%) followed by haircare and bath and body.

According to some interesting data shared by a beauty company, ageing and brightening have become the top concerns for Indian women. Average order value for females stands at **INR** 900 (multiple products) versus an average order value of INR 700 (single product).

* tier: 단계, 층(=row, level)
* INR: Indian rupee. 인도의 화폐단위로 symbol은 ₹

Focus on Grammar

◈ data

K-Beauty regimes are ruling India, claims study *data*

data는 datum의 복수형이므로 일반적 문법 규칙에 따르면 복수동사인 claim을 사용해야 하는데 위 기사에서는 claims를 사용하고 있다. 그런데 일상생활에서의 사용을 보면 data를 단수로 종종 사용한다. 심지어 저명한 신문에서도 단수로 사용하는 예를 볼 수가 있다.

The New York Times 신문은 단/복수로 교차 사용하고 있다. 그 예로 "the survey data are still being analyzed" 와 "the first year for which data is available" 표현을 이틀에 걸쳐(2009년 1월 9일과 10일) 사용하기도 하였다. The Wall Street Journal의 경우 자체 style guide에 두 가지 사용을 명시적으로 허락하고 있다. The Associated Press는 다음과 같은 style guide를 택하고 있다: data를 하나의 단위(unit)로 다룰 때는 단수동사를 사용하고, 개별적인 것들의 모음으로 여길 때는 복수동사를 사용한다. 예, "The data is sound" and "The data have been carefully collected".

Cambridge Dictionary와 Oxford Dictionary 또한 일상의 표준 영어에서 단수동사와 함께 사용하는 셀 수 없는 명사(noncount noun)로 data가 광범위하게 사용되고 있다고 기술하고 있다.

Homegrown beauty and personal care brand, **Pilgrim**, which claims to make borderless beauty experiences accessible and affordable, revealed interesting insights on India's love for global beauty regimes. The company registered a 2X increase in sales in the last 9 months. The sales have primarily been driven by the K-Beauty **range** followed by the French Beauty range. Interestingly, 30% of these sales came from North East India alone with Guwahati leading the **pack**. In metros, Bangalore and Delhi registered maximum sales.

The data also shows that the demand for global beauty products was highest in the 'face care' category with a sales contribution of 80%. The top concerns in these categories were ageing and brightening. With 70% of women buying these global beauty products, the average order value stood at INR 900. This number stood at INR 700 for men who bought one product at a time as compared to females who bought multiple products **in one go**.

source: www.youtube.com

* Pilgrim: 인도 화장품 브랜드. 한국산 원료로 다양한 제품군을 생산하여 자사 브랜드를 붙여 판매.
* range: 제품군(=a number of things in the same category)
* pack: 집단
* in one go: 한번에(=all at one time)

Commenting on the trends, Gagandeep Makker, Co-Founder & COO, Pilgrim, said, "There is an increased inclination towards beauty and personal care in Indian millennials. They want to explore and experience global beauty regimes from the comfort of their homes. Hence, we have seen demand for K-Beauty products increase since we started operations. In fact, we have witnessed an **ARR** of INR 18 **crores** since May 2020. However, there is an appetite for borderless beauty experiences from across the globe, to try out varied regimes. The trend is not a metro phenomenon but also prevalent in smaller cities. So, as a **D2C** brand, we are driven to empower modern millennials with global and affordable beauty rituals at the click of a button."

As per the data, women mostly bought night serums, night gel creams, and face creams. Males on the other hand preferred face wash, face masks, hair serums, and sulfate-free shampoos. These global beauty products were most popular amongst the 25-50 age-group driving 50% of Pilgrim's revenue.

* ARR: Annual Recurring Revenue (연간 반복 매출)
* D2C: Direct-to-Customer

"Focus on Terminology"

◆ crore

인도, 파키스탄, 방글라데시, 네팔 등에서 사용하는 단위로 1 crore는 10 million과 같다. 약어는 cr로 표기. 예) 120 million rupees is 12 crore rupees.

인도의 numbering system (comma의 위치에 유의)

International		Indian	
thousand	1,000	1,000	one thousand
hundred thousand	100,000	1,00,000	one lakh
million	1,000,000	10,00,000	ten lakhs
ten million	10,000,000	1,00,00,000	one crore
billion	1,000,000,000	1,00,00,00,000	one hundred crore
trillion	1,000,000,000,000	10,00,00,00,00,000	one lakh crore

한국산 원료로 인도에서 생산한 Pilgrim face cream 구매 후기

source: www.discoverpilgrim.com

★★★★★	Oh, this is the perfect day cream one can have! 😊 Pretty packaging (well... matters a lot to me), amazing texture, makes your skin look fresh and glowing immediately, the right matte I would say as it's not too drying and definitely not oily. Feels light on the skin, smells amazing and SPF 50 is a plus! Much better yet more affordable than the other creams I own. Love it!! Definitely gonna reorder.
	Excellent product! Impressed that manufacturers are able to bring the international beauty range at affordable price! Two in one—moisturizer+sunscreen!
★★★★	It's a nice moisturizer+sunscreen and has a slight tint to it bcz of which it tones up ur skin. Has a really strong fragrance that fades away after a while but some may find it annoying. So if u are fragrance allergic stay away from it. It gonna suit oily, normal and combination skin. Since it is mattifying cream it's not gonna suit dry or maybe sensitive skin types so keep that in mind.
	The fragrance of the cream is awesome. But not suitable for my skin. I have combination skin. Pimples came when I applied ☹. But still love the fragrance.
★★★	It's more like a BB cream than regular cream. I use it with other cream because it makes my skin dry though I own a normal skin. But it's nice, not bad actually.
	This cream is not for oily skin people although it has mentioned for all skin types. And it is very thick and not light so I personally don't like it very much.
★★	Texture is good and scent is bearable. But it makes your skin extremely sticky, sweaty, oily. Good for dry skin only. Quantity is good. Not at all recommend for oily skin.
	Not good for dry skin and makes your face dull. I won't buy it again even in free ...

Google에 검색한 K-Beauty 관련 질문들

What is the best K-beauty brand?
Is K-Beauty safe?
What are K-beauty products?
Which Korean product is best?
How can I get Korean skin?
Is Korean skin care really better?
What makes Korean skin shiny?
What is so special about K-Beauty?
Who is the owner of K-Beauty?
How can I get Korean skin naturally?
Which is the best Korean cream?
What are the 10 steps of Korean skin care?
What is the best Korean whitening product?
Why do Korean women have beautiful complexion?
Which Korean brand toner is the best?
How is Korean skin so flawless?
Does Korean have pimples?
When did K-beauty get popular?
What is K-beauty trend?
How do Koreans do skin care?
What skincare does BTS use?
What is Korean skin?
How can I get Korean lips?

source: www.kbeautyaddiction.com

source: www.nudieglow.com

Q: What is the secret of Korean white skin?

A: Korean women are in awe of the acne-free and flawless skin. Their radiant, smooth, and even-toned complexions are picture perfect. Were they born beautiful, with clear and flawless skin? No, these women work hard for their manicured features. They do what it takes to protect and preserve their skin. They also learn to take care of their skin from their childhood. For Korean women, skincare is a vital investment, and they spend time and money pampering it.

◇ 다음 단어들을 사용하여 빈 칸을 채워봅시다.

impervious routine adverse perennial options reaction deserves buzzing

This understated K-beauty ingredient is perfect for sensitive skin

One of the toughest skin types to deal with is sensitive skin. One has to be particularly careful while apply products and even DIY recipes that are considered to be less harmful, according to the popular opinion, can actually cause __________ effects on sensitive skin. Any __________ can manifest as rosacea, eczema, **psoriasis**, or dark spots.

While there are dozens of beauty ingredients that can be perfect for sensitive skin, there is an untouched treasure that has remained __________ to the majority of internet bloggers. With Korean skincare being at the **subliminal** level in the market right now, the one ingredient that is __________ currently is mugwort.

This understated ingredient is trending in K-beauty. Mugwort is a __________ plant native to Asia and Northern Europe and can be found in North America too. Amidst a range of soothing __________ like grapeseed oil, **colloidal oatmeal**, and **niacinamide**, mugwort, which has an **unassuming** name, actually __________ much more attention. It is regarded for its healing properties and anti-inflammatory and soothing benefits and should definitely be added to your skincare __________.

* psoriasis [səˈraɪəsɪs]: 건선
* subliminal: 부지불식간에 영향을 미치는(=operating below the threshold of consciousness)
* colloidal oatmeal: 곱게 분쇄한 오트밀
* niaciamide: 수용성 비타민 B3의 구성요소
* unassuming: 건방지지 않은, 겸손한 → 발음하기 어려운 단어/이해하기 어려운 화학 용어가 아님을 우회적으로 표현.

< Famous Quotes About Beauty >

Ⓠ The beauty of a woman must be seen from in her eyes, because that is the doorway to her heart, the place where love resides. — Audrey Hepburn

Ⓠ Beauty is when you can appreciate yourself. When you love yourself, that's when you're most beautiful. — Zoe Kravitz

Ⓠ I need to see my own beauty and to continue to be reminded that I am enough, that I am worthy of love without effort, that I am beautiful, that the texture of my hair and that the shape of my curves, the size of my lips, the color of my skin, and the feelings that I have are all worthy and okay. — Tracee Ellis Ross

Ⓠ Smiling is definitely one of the best beauty remedies. If you have a good sense of humor and a good approach to life, that's beautiful. — Rashida Jones

Ⓠ Life isn't always really glamorous and fabulous. It's about encouraging people to go back to natural beauty. — Zoe Foster Blake

Ⓠ Though we travel the world over to find the beautiful, we must carry it with us or we find it not. — Ralph Waldo Emerson

Ⓠ Beauty of whatever kind, in its supreme development, invariably excites the sensitive soul to tears. — Edgar Allan Poe

Ⓠ It's the imperfections that make things beautiful. — Jenny Han

Ⓠ There is nothing more beautiful than someone who goes out of their way to make life beautiful for others. — Mandy Hale

Ⓠ Makeup is not a mask that covers up your beauty; it's a weapon that helps you express who you are from the inside. — Michelle Phan

Ⓠ You can be gorgeous at thirty, charming at forty, and irresistible for the rest of your life. — Coco Chanel

Ⓠ Strangeness is a necessary ingredient in beauty. — Charles Baudelaire

Ⓠ And in her smile I see something more beautiful than the stars. — Beth Revis

Ⓠ Outer beauty attracts, but inner beauty captivates. — Kate Angell

Cross-word Puzzle

ACROSS

4. to spread something thickly on
7. one that performs more than one function
8. any group that associates together
9. a period of illness
10. to peel off
14. tending to reform
15. not arrogant or boastful
16. an effort to resist

DOWN

1. to dip or splash in a liquid
2. a person's state of mind
3. to immerse in liquid for a long time
5. excessively charged
6. a poisonous fluid
11. a firm basis
12. destroying the growth of fungi
13. to remove harmful chemicals from

Chapter VI

K-FASHION

Five emerging Korean designer labels driving K-fashion's international expansion: Rokh, MINJUKIM and other designer labels are at the forefront of the influential, home-grown Korean talent developing the hallyu **narrative in a similar vein** to K-beauty, K-pop and K-movies

K-fashion is dynamic. Bold yet balanced, colourful but tasteful, edgy and sophisticated—making it a challenge to define, but attractive and easy to buy. You can find any style you want in Seoul, South Korea's international fashion capital. Mega outlets with endless streetwear coupled with **curated** boutiques selling the latest styles by talented, emerging designers. Korean fashion is influential, and a big reason for that energy stems from the home-grown talent trying to express the hallyu narrative through innovation and creativity. Here are five up-and-coming designer labels to look out for:

MINJUKIM

source: www.newsweek.com

Designer Minju Kim has gained prominence after winning the first season of *Next in Fashion*, Netflix's fashion design competition show.

* designer label: 유명한 디자이너의 상품(=brand)
* narrative: 메시지
* in a similar vein: 같은 맥락에서
* curated: 체계적이고 관리된(=organized and overseen)

Week after week, Kim **wowed** judges with designs displaying exceptional craftsmanship and an eye for voluminous silhouettes as exemplified by her showstopping hanbok-like, **ethereal** wedding dress as part of her finale showcase. Kim has an eye for a pretty, romantic, feminine dress that is approachable and **flattering for women of all body types**. There is something inclusive about her collections, building volume with **Victorian inspirations** while keeping her clothes modern, dreamy and comfortable. Think big coats, **bustling** skirts, **peplum dresses** and **bubbly** jackets with dangling ribbons.

source: www.net-a-porter.com

* wow: 깊은 인상을 주다, 열광시키다
* ethereal: 가녀린(=extremely light or delicate)
* flattering for women of all body types: 모든 체형의 여성들을 만족시키는
* bustling: 요란한
* peplum dress: 허리 아래 짧은 주름 장식이 있는 드레스
* bubbly: 넉넉한, 활기찬(=lively, animated)

"Focus on Terminology"

◆ Victorian inspiration

19세기 말에 유행했던 Victorian fashion에서 얻은 영감. 그 당시 스타일은 여성성을 강조하였다. 주요 특징으로 화려한 직물(luxurious fabric)의 사용, 코르셋 등을 이용하여 아름다운 실루엣을 강조, 노출을 절제하는 단정함(modesty), 화려한 액세서리 등을 꼽을 수 있다.

Kim holds two degrees—one from SADI, the Samsung Art & Design Institute, and another from the Royal Academy of Fine Arts Antwerp where she studied under the great Walter Van Beirendonck. His influence is apparent when it comes to her colour and **whimsical** prints. Kim also won the **H&M Design Award** in 2013 and the LVMH Prize for Young Fashion Designers in 2015. She has designed for K-pop artists such as boy band BTS.

GODSOMWARE

"If you build it, they will come", is the **mantra** behind Aggie Nam's facial accessory brand. Facial accessory, not eyewear, because none of Nam's designs has any functional purpose. It's all purely aesthetic-driven. It was a kind of spiritual **calling**, an "energy" as she describes it, that forced her to create her series of signature "butterfly sunglasses", which cover the face with carefully positioned acrylic pieces shaped like insect wings.

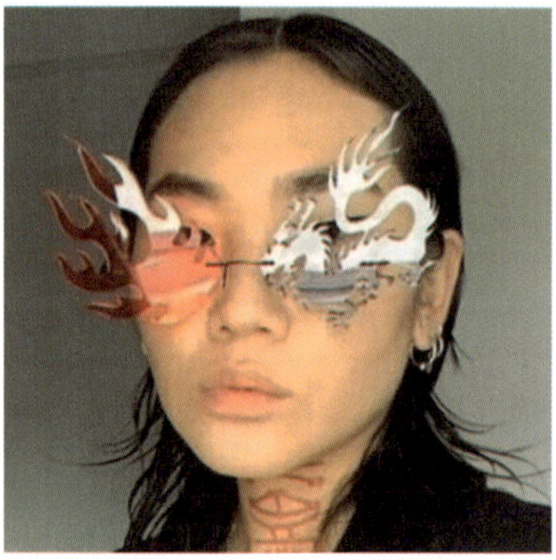

source: www.dazeddigital.com

* whimsical: 엉뚱한, 기발한
* mantra: 반복 사용하는 문구
* calling: 충동(=impulse)

"Focus on Terminology"

◆ H&M Design Award

Sweden의 의류회사인 Hennes & Mauritz AB가 패션 산업에 발을 들여 놓는 젊은 디자이너들을 지원하기 위해 수여하는 상이다. 전 세계 42개 design school의 학, 석사 졸업자가 지원할 수 있다. 우승자에게는 €50,000의 상금과 Stockholm에 있는 H&M 본사에서 6개월 동안의 인턴 자격이 주어진다. 2013년 Minju Kim이 Royal Academy of Fine Arts in Antwerp 학사 졸업 작품집으로 수상하였다.

Some of the accessories are like eyewear, others cover the face like a mask, providing a sense of theatre and performance. Other design shapes include fierce electric flames, a giant heart and a black dragon. Janelle Monáe wore Nam's "Third Eye Protection" to a **Met Gala** after-party like some ancient mystic.

Nam's designs blend the natural and religious worlds. In an **i-D** interview, Nam said the name of the brand means "God that exists somewhere, a thing that occurred as God insisted, and I got it from somewhere". Nam, an atheist, is inspired by other-worldly things, and fans love her for it. The brand has built up a considerable following which loves to wear Nam's striking accessories on Instagram.

* i-D: 패션 잡지 이름

"Focus on Terminology"

◈ Met Gala

뉴욕시에 있는 Metropolitan Museum of Art's Costume Institute를 위한 기금모음 행사로 1948년에 최초로 개최됨. 매년 5월 첫 번째 월요일에 열리는데 *Vogue*에서 주관하며 Costume Institute의 연례 패션 전시의 시작을 기념함. Costume Institute Gala, Costume Institute Benefit, 또는 Met Ball이라고 부른다. 또한 'Fashion's biggest night out'이란 애칭을 가지고 있다.

source: www.today.com

CHANCECHANCE

The menswear label, launched by Kim Chan in 2013, exemplifies Korean streetwear excellence blended with a sense of dandy and punk. The brand, which draws on many influences, is **endorsed** by many Korean influencers, including boy band BTS. Chan's latest collection is a colourful, multitextured one that uses various technical fabrics. There are high-waisted punk trousers, an oversized peach blazer with matching shirt, checkered skinny trousers and vest, a **faux** fur check jacket, a glossy moss green trench, bubbly bomber jackets, and an American flag quilted cape. Everything in the collection can be incorporated into an everyday wardrobe.

source: www.naver.com

bomber jacket. source: www.lineblog.me

* endorse: 지지하다, 보증하다
* faux: 모조의(=artificial)

Focus on Terminology

◆ bomber jacket

미국 공군 조종사들이 입는 flight jacket의 한 종류로 허리길이의 짧은 상의를 응용하여 디자인한 것으로, 주로 양가죽으로 만든 가죽 재킷을 지칭한다. bomber는 '폭격기'를 뜻하는데 세계대전 때 공군 조종사들이 입었던 재킷들이 여러 변화를 거쳐 오늘날의 모습을 지니게 되었다.

Rokh

Korean-born designer Rok Hwang has created quite a **buzz** since winning the LVHM Special Prize in 2018, and debuting at Paris Fashion Week in 2019. Before starting his own label, Rokh, he spent three years at Céline under the **tutelag**e of Phoebe Philo, and spent time freelancing for Chloe and Louis Vuitton. Today he has around 100 **stockists** and has a loyal customer fan base.

source: www.edition-jp.com

In some ways, Hwang is filling the gap that Philo left behind when you notice the cuts of his clothes. His perspective when it comes to deconstruction, colour and adaptable details makes him stand out. His signatures include his trench coats cut, tailored and adapted in as many ways as possible, luxurious leather jackets and accessories, and **impeccably** tailored trousers and blazers for working women. Hwang works with an all-female staff at his London studio, and designs with sustainability in mind.

* buzz: 관심(=excited interest, attention)
* tutelage: 지도, 후견(=guardianship)
* stockist: 판매점(=a retailer that stocks merchandize)
* impeccably: 완벽하게

MÜNN

Established in 2013, MÜNN is a unisex label that continues to impress with smart cuts and a balanced blend of streetwear and deconstructed formal wear. Designer Han Hyun-min is known for his **wool and selvedge suiting**, but in his latest show at London Fashion Week he showed his range and ability to innovate with pieces like his woven cape made out of men's ties.

source: www.munnseoul.kr

The autumn/winter 2020 collection was filled with detailed clothes like an oversized, **asymmetrical** pinstripe blazer/coat hybrid or a long coat with a flowing scarf tail. Every outfit **married** numerous textures, fabrics and accessories, yet there is still a sense of clear intent and polish with each look, even with zips placed in all directions on a silver nylon jacket and pants set.

* wool and selvedge suiting: wool과 가장자리를 옷감으로 활용한 의상
* asymmetrical: 비대칭의(↔ symmetrical)
* marry: 결합하다, 통합하다

◇ 다음 단어와 반대의 의미를 지닌 단어를 위 글에서 찾아봅시다.

1. nonspecific 2. cease (v.) 3. obscure
4. separate (v.) 5. disproportioned 6. casual

< Big four fashion weeks of the world >

A fashion week is a fashion industry event, lasting about a week, where fashion designers, brands or "houses" display their latest collections in runway fashion shows to buyers and the media. These events influence trends for the current and upcoming seasons. The most prominent fashion weeks are held in the fashion capitals of the world; Paris, Milan, London and New York, which are called the "Big Four." Each of the fashion weeks is held twice a year, usually in February for fall/winter collections and September for spring/summer collections. Fashion week events begin with New York, followed by London, and then Milan and end in Paris.

New York Fashion Week	Generally lasting 7 to 9 days twice a year, the purpose of the events are to showcase American fashions, which ordinarily play a secondary role to French designs. The first NY fashion week was held in 1943.
London Fashion Week	It shows over 250 global designers to a media and retailer influence. It isn't available to the general public but there is a festival for 4 days at the end of the fashion week, called London Fashion Week Festival, which fashionistas and the general public can go too.
Milan Fashion Week	Milan fashion week includes more than 40 shows each season and transforms the city into a touristic target by simply creating various venues for the shows. They select the most elegant and influential palaces to become the stage for design. Examples of location are Palazzo Reale, Palazzo Serbelloni and many others.
Paris Fashion Week	A series of designer presentations held semiannually with spring/summer and autumn/winter events each year. Famous brands like Dior, Chanel, Louis Vuitton, Givenchy, and Céline host their shows in historical places such as the Carrousel du Louvre and the Grand Palais. The first Paris Fashion Week was held in October 1973. The event was a fundraiser held at the Palace of Versailles to restore the palace.

< Fashion show terminology >

3-to-1 shuffle	원래 지정 좌석이 세 번째 줄인 관객이 show가 시작할 무렵에 첫 번째 줄로 옮기는 행위
a la mode	fashion을 뜻하는 불어 표현
cattle call	다수의 모델이 참석하는 group interview
composite (card)/ SED card	모델을 홍보하기 위해 개인 정보와 사진 등을 포함한 카드
de rigueur	required by fashion
dresser	model이 옷을 바꿔 입을 때 도와주는 사람
first look	show 시작 전에 designer가 자신의 model이 의도대로 의상을 갖추었는지 확인하는 것
flaunt	자랑스럽게 보여주다
frow	front row
glad rags	멋진 의상
glitterati	a group of attractive and stylish people
haute couture	upscale and exclusive custom-fitting clothes
minaudière	runway에 모델들이 가끔 들고 나오는 hard, box-shaped clutches
newfangled	(불필요하게) 특이한
passé	유행이 지난
prêt-à-porter	ready-to-wear clothing
rag trade	의류 산업
riser	runway 끝 부분의 약간 높은 곳. riser 앞에 사진 기자들이 몰려들어 최고의 사진을 얻으려고 함.
run of show	fashion show의 모든 진행 절차 목록
runway/catwalk/ramp	fashion show에서 모델들이 걸어가는 좁은 통로
show notes	collection의 중요 아이디어를 적은 노트로 fashion show에 참석하면 의자에 놓여 있음
smock frock	드레스 위에 입는 헐렁한 옷
swag bag	관객들에게 주는 홍보용 샘플을 담은 가방

1. 다음의 단어들을 사용하여 빈 칸을 채워봅시다.

references rise cements historic forefront viral

You could say South Korea has had an influence on global pop culture, but that would be a massive understatement. In fact, the country's pop culture ascendency has been so __________ there's even a unique term that describes its impact on so many areas of how we live today: Hallyu—also known as the Korean Wave. If you've taken note of the __________ in Korean beauty, film, television, and music, you've already experienced the effect of Hallyu, which further __________ the East Asian country's position as a world power. Names like Bong Joon Ho and BTS are at the __________ of the entertainment industry, while brands like Soko Glam lead the beauty world. And with these examples as __________, it feels as though Korean culture is leaving a molten gold path of modern culture and __________ popularity in its wake. While more and more of the world turns its eyes towards the country, there's another area on which it's putting its Midas touch: fashion.

2. 괄호 안 단어를 활용하여 적절한 표현으로 빈 칸을 채워봅시다.

a. As the winner of Netflix's reality competition series *Next in Fashion*, designer Minju Kim had a chance to introduce her eponymous brand to a global market, including the opportunity to ____________ (stock) on NET-A-PORTER.
b. Nam's designs are abstract in execution but ____________ (ostensible) basic in conception, which is essentially part of the appeal.
c. Most fashion critics feel Rok Hwang has an ____________ (aesthetics) clothing style that may very well fill the gap left by Phoebe Philo's departure from 'old Céline.'
d. Every outfit of MÜNN's autumn/winter 2020 collection ____________ (carry) a wide range of textures, fabrics, and accessories; yet there is a sense of intent and polished look.

London Has Fallen In Love With South Korean Fashion

London, Paris, New York and Milan have been synonymous with high-end fashion for decades, known for their fashion weeks and household name brands. Now, South Korea, and more specifically Seoul, wants a slice of the action too.

In the last five years, Korean brands such as JUUN.J, ADER error and, more recently, WE11DONE have become **mainstays** in the streetwear sphere thanks to not only the rising influence of K-pop and TikTok, but also these brands' consistent collaborations with more established streetwear names. This year alone, we've seen ADER error team up with Alpha Industries and Maison Kitsuné; **thisisneverthat** has delivered numerous **capsules** with New Balance; and Hyein Seo's collaboration with Woo, and its own **stellar** Fall/Winter 2020 collection, prove the brand is just getting started.

South Korean labels are on the global fashion map in 2020—and many of them can be found in some of London's best up-and-coming stores. Sure, you can find more established labels in historic retailers throughout the city, but there's a lot more to South Korea's fashion output than the big names.

* mainstay: 핵심(=keystone), 정신적 지주(=anchor)
* thisisneverthat: 한국 의류 브랜드
* capsule: 대표적인 제품(=an important representative item)
* stellar: 뛰어난(=outstanding)

Tokyo-born store XU London, founded by Riri Tabuchi, is just one such example. With both established labels like **archival** COMME des GARÇONS, Sacai and Yohji Yamamoto, as well as emerging Korean brands such as CRANK and ANOTHER YOUTH, it's a melting pot of newness, perfect for those who want something no one else will have.

London's UJNG, operated by Usman Zia and Jasmin Meyer, curates a selection of designers from all around the world with a focus on Asian brands, including a prominent roster of South Korean labels. Alongside the likes of 1017 ALYX 9SM, MM6 Maison Margiela, and C2H4 are brands such as WE11DONE, Andersson Bell, IISE, JUUN.J, JIWON YUN, and many other big-name and emerging Korean brands — most of which are selling out.

"WE11DONE is already the next [big brand from South Korea], we can see it from the data in-store and online—it has a growing following. If you read any magazine or blog you can't miss it, it has become Asia and international celebrities' favorite—G Dragon and Justin Bieber. It has its own style, premium fabrics, and a cool aesthetic," notes UJNG's Zia.

* archival: 역사가 있는. cf. COMME des GARÇONS label은 1969년에 등장함.

Focus on Vocabulary

◆ likes

Alongside the *likes* of 1017 ALYX 9SM, MM6 Maison Margiela, and C2H4 are brands such as ... .

명사로서 'like'는 informal English에서 '유사한 것/사람(similar person/ thing)'을 뜻하며 주로 복수형 'likes'로 쓰인다. 위 문장의 뜻은 다음과 같다: '1017 ALYX 9SM, MM6 Maison Margiela, and C2H4 같은 brands와 나란히 (such as 이하에서 열거한) brand 제품들이 진열되어있다.' 즉, 한국 brand들이 다른 나라의 알려진 brand들과 어깨를 나란히 한다는 의미.

For XU London, Tabuchi is noticing that people appreciate what emerging South Korean labels have to offer, and not because of their connections to the likes of G Dragon. "Korean fashion has some elements that non-Korean fashion [brands] don't have, such as functionality and detail. Some people say Korean brands started rising thanks to K-pop, but I don't really think so. It's just that people **organically** started noticing it and understanding its value. Customers come to the store because they like detail or oversized designs—not because they like K-pop," says Tabuchi.

While oversized garments or **embellishments** are nothing new, those elements have often been exclusive to a high-end clientele. **On the flip side**, Korean fashion comes in at a more affordable price point, which "really tapped into the mood of the consumer," as Zia says. He adds, "They focus on **timeless** quality clothing in fresh clean colors. The silhouettes are usually oversized and look good on all body shapes, which makes them appealing to all types of shoppers. Also **with times being as uncertain as they are**, shoppers are increasingly price-conscious which makes Korean brands very competitive."

Because of their affordability and trend appeal, Korean fashions have captured the attention of London's youth. As such, London's younger generation is turning to smaller independent brands from Korea to stand out in a **streetwear-centric** crowd that's still obsessed with **cultish** names.

* organically: 기본적으로
* embellishment: 장식물(=ornament)
* on the flip side: 다른 한편으로는
* timeless: 유행을 타지 않는
* with times being as uncertain as they are: 시기적으로 사회 상황이 불확실한 것처럼, 소비자들이 (옷을) 사야할지 말아야할지 불확실할 때
* streetwear-centric: 스트리트 패션 중심의
* cultish: 숭배하는(=appealing to a small group of fashionable people)

"I think people who love streetwear fashion started to get a little bit bored of [existing] fashion brands, so the timing has been very good for those people who are seeking new fashion from somewhere," says Tabuchi. Streetwear as we've known it has for years centered on overt branding, **hype-driven** design and status symbols. On one hand, Korean fashion avoids this **branded** approach—pieces such as ANOTHERYOUTH's faux leather blazer is minimally **emblazoned** and focuses much more on garment execution—yet at the same time, the country's fashion industry does also have status symbols in its influencers.

source: www.anotheryouth.com

"To me, it looks like the younger generation places much more value on quality or design than on just a brand's name value. I've seen a lot of people being happy with Korean brands offering them new styles with good prices, because they know some of the non-Korean brands offer them the same style over and over again. It's design and detail, and not about the fashion name," adds Tabuchi.

* hype-driven: (광고나 홍보효과를 노리고) 과장된, 지나치게 화려한
* branded: (logo등을 두드러지게 하여) 브랜드를 강조하는
* emblazoned: (글자나 그림을) 두드러지게 새긴

Focus on Grammar

◈ 지각동사 (see) + 목적어 + 원형동사/동사-ing

I've *seen* a lot of people *being* happy with Korean brands offering them new styles with good prices ...

주어가 목적어(a lot of people)의 행동/상태를 목격할 때 그 것이 '목격 순간에 진행되고 있는지' 아니면 '평소에 그러한지'의 의미차이에 관계없이 '원형동사'나 '동사-ing'를 사용할 수 있다.

People are starting to pay attention to Korean labels, and arguably, they have no choice but to. As we've touched on already, Korean fashion brands are being worn, designed, or promoted by some of the country's most famous exports, dominating social media where youth culture and fashion breed. "The new fashion crowd is a lot more aware and researches labels. We have a lot of people coming in-store already knowing about the new up-and-coming Korean designers. Korean brands have a lot of hype on Instagram and this comes from the huge K-pop influence. Korea has the music and movies and that's all filtering into promoting their brands," says Zia.

Those interested in Korean fashion brands are onto something bigger than tapping **niche** luxury labels from the West. For many young consumers, it's not about how good of quality or how rare your Carol Christian Poell boots and hard-to-find Raf Simons is anymore. It's about being a **vanguard**. Korean fashion recognizes this, as Zia says: "[Korean fashion brands] are also the first to deliver, so the new collection is in-store first—in a world of fast fashion being first does count."

source: www.carolchristianpoell.com

And that model is **conducive** to the London audience. "London has always been very accepting of new trends, and is proud to be a very fashion-forward city," UJNG's founders add. "The youth of London is very informed and the Korean Fashion scene has been on their radar for some time. Now that stores like us are stocking them, the customers have a point of the purchase to touch and feel the fabric. The number of Korean brands being worn on the streets of London is definitely increasing."

* niche: 확실한, 두드러진(=distinct)
* vanguard: 선두주자(=forefront)
* conducive (to): ~에 도움이 되는(=contributing)

And the names being worn on the street aren't just the K-Pop-pushed streetwear labels. "London has always been more style-driven and less star-influenced. The Korean scene is heavily influenced by K-Pop but we see simpler brands such as Andersson Bell performing at the same level as K-Pop-influenced brands such as WE11DONE," adds Zia. Tabuchi agrees, adding "Most consumers buy Korean brands simply because they're interested in them or they admire the style they offer them," and that it "gives us an experience more than the value costs."

Experience is everything when it comes to Korean fashion. Streetwear brands are **a dime a dozen** in London (and throughout the West). In contrast, outside of their home country, Korean brands are somewhat limited to specialist stores such as UJNG and XU London. Coupled with quality-driven, trend-setting and often limited production runs—as well as the price-points—these brands offer an entirely new experience to customers. One that feels exclusive, but is in fact inclusive: buying into Korean fashion gives the illusion of exclusivity, but thanks to its affordability and altered sense of familiarity, it's something we can all **tap into**.

* tap into: 잘 활용하다

Focus on Vocabulary

◆ a dime a dozen

Streetwear brands are *a dime a dozen* in London (and throughout the West).

'a dime a dozen' 표현은 1800년대에 미국에서 '(달걀이나 오렌지 같은) 동일 물건 12개를 a dime (10 cents)'에 판매할 때 사용하던 표현이다. 즉, 당시 그 물건들은 흔한 것들이었다. 20세기 들어 '특정 물건/사람이 너무 흔해서(common) 값어치가 거의 없는(valueless) 것'을 지칭하는 비유적인 표현으로 널리 쓰이게 되었다. 영국 영어에서는 같은 의미를 지닌 표현으로 'two a penny' 'ten a penny'가 있다.

WE11DONE hoodie 구입 후기

source: www.farfetch.com

First up, I have never seen one in real life. So I can only compare it to the shots on the We11done website.

Quality: The quality is great, stitching is clean and all the details are also looking to be right. The tags are clean printed.

The Backprint with the 3D applicated zipper (오른쪽 사진의 화살표 가리키는 곳) is also feeling really nice, but I have to check how long it holds with wear/washes. The weight is also nice. Not too heavy and not too light in my opinion. But, the black tag on the back is stitched so **wonky**. They should pay more attention to this, nothing which is major, but you really just need to follow the black line^^ 8.5/10 just because it is good, but I am not 100% **blown away**.

Accuracy: The drawstrings and the color seem to be correct and also the details like the zipper on the back or the black name tag. Print size may be a bit small, but this could be due to the photos or the way I laid the hoodie on the ground. 9.5/10

Fit: This thing is huge, but the fit is really nice and it wears nice.

* wonky: 정렬이 안 된(=out of alignment)
* blow away: 완전히 압도하다(=overwhelm)

Will K-fashion take off in the US?

K-Fashion is **gaining traction** in the states.

Timed with its 10-year anniversary, South Korean fashion brand Greedilous launched in the U.S. last month via a direct-to-consumer site that sells its made-to-order styles. It marks the first time the brand has been available to U.S. shoppers, despite that it's shown at New York Fashion Week, collaborated with popular U.S. brands, and been worn by celebrities including Cardi B and Beyoncé.

GREEDILOUS
P.Y.H

source: www.greedilous.com

According to founder and designer YounHee Park, she was advised to explore and expand to the U.S. market by a top Japanese buyer "because of the Hollywood influence." Park said she plans to incorporate the brand's celebrity fans in its local marketing. In addition to American stars, they include actress Sandara Park, formerly of K-Pop band 2NE1, and Korean model Gabi Moon.

Kayla Marci, market analyst at retail data company Edited, said that Korean celebrities are becoming increasingly influential in the states. The popularity of K-dramas, now streaming on apps including Netflix, is expected to transition to the Western market, much like K-pop and K-beauty in recent years.

* gain traction: 인기를 끌다, 호응을 얻다

"With the events of 2020 disrupting the traditional trend **funnel**, retailers and consumers have been drawing trend inspiration from other mediums such as music videos and viral series on streaming services," said Marci.

Overall, K-fashion has been **catching on**, particularly among streetwear fans, who have for years **scooped up** unique pieces by brands including PushButton and Adererror. **LVMH**-backed L Catterton invested in Korean eyewear brand Gentle Monster in 2017, and more recently, Seoul Fashion Week has attracted global attention rivaling that of the **four fashion capitals**.

But considering Greedilous' styles are far from trendy loungewear, the expansion could still prove ill-timed. Unlike the many fashion brands that have launched casual apparel categories since March, Greedlious has remained relatively focused on its bright statement pieces. According to Park, Greedilous was, however, the first Korean brand to make printed masks to match its ready-to-wear styles. And the timing isn't a concern, she said.

source: www.greedilous.com

"During this pandemic, the desires for self-exploration and -expression seem [stronger] than ever, and I am happy to continue sharing designs that empower people to communicate and express themselves without fear," she said, via a translator. Indeed, there's evidence that bright clothes have sparked joy for consumers during the pandemic.

* funnel: 전달 경로, 창구
* catch on: 인기를 끌다(=become popular)
* scoop up: 주워 담다, 집어들다
* LVMH: LVMH Moët Hennessy Louis Vuitton
* four fashion capitals: London, Milan, New York and Paris

The brand's original U.S. launch plan, with physical components, was **derailed** due to the pandemic, said Park. So she's currently focused on building its local online and social media presence, and exploring ways to virtually communicate with local shoppers. Greedilous currently has 25,000 Instagram followers. Gaining awareness through a fashion marketplace or multi-brand **e-tailer** wasn't an option, she said.

"Selling directly to the consumer allows us to have full control of our brand image and gain a better understanding of our customer in the U.S.," said Park. "We hope to use the [resulting] insights to offer better service and support, strengthen brand loyalty, and build stronger relationships with existing and potential customers."

* e-tailer: 온라인 소매업체

"Focus on Vocabulary"

◆ prefix (접두사) de-

The brand's original U.S. launch plan, with physical components, was *derailed* due to the pandemic, said Park.

prefix de-는 제거(removal), 분리(separation), 부정(negation), 하락(descent) 등의 뜻을 지니고 있다. 위 문장에서는 '분리'의 의미를 부여하는 경우로 'derail'은 '원래의 궤도 또는 계획에서 벗어남'을 뜻한다.

◇ 문맥에 맞는 단어의 올바른 형태로 빈 칸을 채워봅시다.

deflect detach defrost degrade deactivate

1. Every day the environment is __________ by toxic wastes.
2. The facility will __________ any drones that get too close to the area.
3. It helps them __________ themselves from the problem and become more objective.
4. The crowd cheered as the goalkeeper __________ the shot.
5. Park your car facing east to __________ the windshield in the morning.

According to Polly Wong, president of marketing and creative agency Belardi Wong, international brands are increasingly opting to launch **stateside** by way of **DTC** channels. "They're building DTC in the U.S. for the same reason wholesale brands are [now] building DTC in the U.S. People are starting to realize the power of the customer relationship," she said. "If your customer buys your product in Amazon, you never really build a relationship with them—and having a marketing customer database is a tremendous asset to a company. When you can continue to re-market directly to that consumer, you drive up their lifetime value and you drive up the profit of the company."

Greedilous' U.S. e-commerce site is simply the Korean site updated to feature English copy and local currency. As the brand doesn't have a local warehouse, orders will ship from Seoul, arriving to U.S. shoppers in 2-3 days via FedEx, **EMS** or **Master Air**. Park is currently seeking a local web developer to take the site to the next level, with more imagery, for example.

* stateside: 미국 내에
* DTC: Direct To Customer
* EMS: Express Mail Service
* Master Air: 항공택배 전문회사

◇ 다음 빈 칸에 가장 적절한 단어를 위 글에서 찾아 채워봅시다.

1. The walkways and riverside areas are very attractive and a great ____________ to the town.
2. ____________ is a large building where raw materials or manufactured goods are stored.
3. The holiday was cancelled so the travel ____________ had to refund everybody the price of the tickets.
4. Tape recordings of conversations are transcribed by typists and entered into the ____________.
5. Should Britain abandon the pound and join the European single ____________?
6. This year the airline will be hard-pressed to make a ____________.

In February 2018, Greedilous styles walked the runway at New York Fashion Week through Concept Korea, the government-sponsored fashion show aimed at promoting global awareness of Korean designers. Park said the show drove interest from U.S. buyers and celebrities, **the latter of which** shopped the styles and fueled awareness and "rocketed" sales in Korea. Beyoncé bought an entire rack of Greedilous clothes in NYC, according to Park.

source: www.thesun.co.uk

Also helping to market the brand are its regular collaborations with Barbie, Givenchy Beauty, Prada Eyewear and Paris Hilton, among others. Since launching in 2009, the brand has collaborated on 36 collections in Korea. Park said it's a strategy she plans to continue in the U.S.

Park self-funded the brand until 2019, when she became one of five designers to receive a government grant from the National (Korean) Designer Fund. She said investors have come knocking, but she's passed as she disagreed with their ideas for the company's direction.

* the latter of which: 관계절 앞의 선행사가 U.S. buyers와 celebrities 두 명사인데 latter는 celebrities를 지칭

In 2016, Greedilous expanded into menswear after Park noticed men buying pieces from the line—it's made up of the same styles in men's sizes. Three years later, she launched Yunni G., a sub-brand targeting a younger **demographic**.

Moving forward, Park wants to grow Greedilous to become a large unisex brand, reaching Chanel status. A couture line is in the brand's future, she said, especially as she sees it as an extension of the current on-demand manufacturing model. Greedilous currently employs eight people and four freelancers who specialize in pattern-making and production.

source: www.greedilous.com

* demographic: (소비자 같은) 특정 인구 집단

Focus on Terminology

◈ Types of Manufacturing

- OBM (Original Brand Manufacturing): 기업이 자체 브랜드를 가지고 직접 디자인과 생산, 유통 그리고 마케팅까지 수행하는 방식을 말한다.
- OEM (Original Equipment Manufacturing): 기업이 자체 브랜드를 가지고 제조, 판매하기 이전에 그 분야에서 앞선 기업의 상품을 위탁 생산하는 경우로 주문자로부터 설계도를 받아 제품을 위탁 생산하는 방식이다.
- ODM (Original Design Manufacturing): 주문자가 건네준 설계도에 따라 단순히 생산만 하는 OEM과 달리 생산 위탁을 받은 제품을 자체 개발, 생산하는 방식이다. 제조업체에서 자체적으로 기술을 개발하기 때문에 부가가치가 높고, 해외로의 판매가 이루어질 경우 개발 로열티(royalty)를 받는 등 고부가가치를 지닌 생산 방식으로 인정받고 있다.

< Creating a brand name >

위 article에서 소개한 Greedilous의 홈페이지에 따르면 Greedilous는 “Greedy (욕심 많은)+Fabulous(아름다운) 단어의 조합으로 ‘미의 여신’을 뜻한다”고 밝히고 있다. 그리고 brand concept는 unique pattern, pattern design, and individuality를 포함하고 있다고 한다. brand name을 지을 때는 이처럼 핵심 concept를 단어로 표현하는 과정을 거치게 된다.

여러분이 의류 회사를 창립한다면 어떤 brand concept와 그에 따른 brand name(s)은 무엇으로 하고 싶은지 적어봅시다.

brand concept:

brand name(s):

여러분이 시계 회사를 창립한다면 어떤 brand concept와 그에 따른 brand name(s)은 무엇으로 하고 싶은지 적어봅시다.

brand concept:

brand name(s):

◇ 아래에 주어진 단어들을 활용하거나, 괄호 안 단어를 활용하여 적절한 표현으로 빈 칸을 채워봅시다.

experiment vary original garment target allotted annual marketable

Fashion Designers: Who are they?

Fashion designers often work for textile companies, clothing manufacturers, or wholesalers that sell clothing online or to retail stores. They use creativity to design new styles for their __________ customers. High-end fashion designers exercise greater creativity to develop innovative, __________ designs. Most fashion designers work in street fashion, where clothing is mass-produced at an __________ (afford) price point. These fashion designers gather inspiration from the previous season's top sellers, runway shows and seasonal trends to design __________ styles for their customers. They choose colors and fabrics and design the number of tops, bottoms and dresses __________ by the inventory planning and merchandising teams. You may enjoy this career if you have a **flair** for fashion and innate __________ (art) ability.

Some fashion designers __________ (hire) by film and video producers to design costumes. Many use computer-aided design, or CAD, programs to __________ with different colors, lines and shapes before selecting fabrics that complement their design. The design is then used to create a __________ that is viewed on a model and modified as __________ (need).

The median __________ salary for fashion designers is $73,790, as of May 2019. Salaries __________ widely. Those in the bottom 10 percent earn less than $37,260, while those in the top 10 percent earn more than $140,010.

* flair: 재능(=talent, knack)

< Famous Quotes About Fashion >

- Don't be into trends. Don't make fashion own you, but you decide what you are, what you want to express by the way you dress and the way to live. — Gianni Versace
- What you wear is how you present yourself to the world, especially today, when human contacts are so quick. Fashion is instant language. — Miuccia Prada
- I don't design clothes. I design dreams. — Ralph Lauren
- I think there is beauty in everything. What 'normal' people perceive as ugly, I can usually see something of beauty in it. — Alexander McQueen
- Fashion is very important. It is life-enhancing and, like everything that gives pleasure, it is worth doing well. — Vivienne Westwood
- You can never take too much care over the choice of your shoes. Too many women think that they are unimportant, but the real proof of an elegant woman is what is on her feet. — Christian Dior
- Shoes transform your body language and attitude. They lift you physically and emotionally. — Christian Louboutin
- In order to be irreplaceable one must always be different. — Coco Chanel
- Elegance is not standing out, but being remembered. — Giorgio Armani
- Fashion is about dressing according to what's fashionable. Style is more about being yourself. — Oscar de la Renta
- You gotta have style. It helps you get down the stairs. It helps you get up in the morning. It's a way of life. Without it, you're nobody. I'm not talking about lots of clothes. — Diana Vreeland
- I always find beauty in things that are odd and imperfect, they are much more interesting. — Marc Jacobs
- Fashion is like eating, you shouldn't stick to the same menu. — Kenzo Takada
- When in doubt, wear red. — Bill Blass
- Fashion is the armor to survive the reality of everyday life. — Bill Cunningham

Cross-word Puzzle

ACROSS

3. the state of being pulled
6. extremely delicate
8. a portion of a population
11. not genuine
12. outstanding
13. adorned with a prominent marking
14. to impress greatly

DOWN

1. organized
2. the act of guiding
4. having no balance
5. spontaneously playful
7. the forefront position in a trend
9. having no flaws
10. full of energetic activity
12. to pick up swiftly

Chapter VII

K-ARTS

Frame At Last: Master's 'Lost' Painting Missing For 45 Years Up For Sale At $850,000

A painting by Korean minimalist painter and sculptor Lee Ufan said to be worth $856,000 has been discovered in an attic in Cognac, France, by an art expert who visited the property to appraise wine.

The French artist who owned the rural farmhouse had known Ufan 45 years earlier, and the pair had swapped some of their work. French auctioneer Emmanuel Layan, who discovered the painting, said the property owner's son mentioned his father was a retired painter with an impressive collection. They went to the attic where the paintings were stored. Layan said he immediately knew the painting was remarkable; the **hunch** was confirmed after spotting Ufan's signature. Research revealed the French artist and Ufan had both been in Paris and in Anvers in 1976, where they had exchanged works. The French artist retired in the 1980s; Ufan has since become well-known. The numbered piece, "From Point (in Paris)," has been valued at between 400,000 and 700,000 euros ($489,000-$856,000). It is set to go on auction in Bordeaux on June 20.

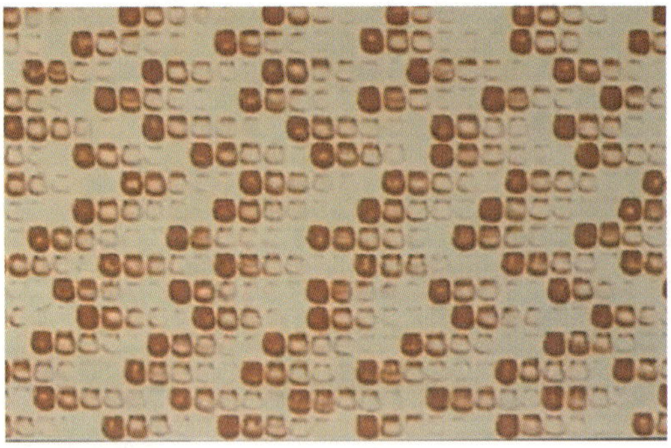

From Point (in Paris). source: www.gazette-drouot.com

Ufan has had worldwide exhibits of his paintings, starting in 1967 in Japan. His "Marking Infinity" exhibition was featured at the Guggenheim Museum in New York City in 2011.

* hunch: 예감(=intuition, feeling)

이우환(Lee Ufan)

- painter, sculptor, and writer born in 1936
- attended Seoul National University and Tokyo's Nihon University. Lee rose to prominence in the late 1960s as the leading theorist and practitioner of Mono-ha (物派), a Japanese art movement that rejected Western notions of representation, focusing on the relationships of materials and perceptions.
- recent exhibitions: Venice Biennale (2007); Guggenheim Museum, New York (2011); Palace of Versailles, France (2014); Hirshhorn Museum and Sculpture Garden, D.C. (2019); Mori Art Museum, Tokyo (2020)
- collections: MOMA, New York; Guggenheim Museum, New York; Centre Georges Pompidou, Paris; Tate Gallery, London; Kröller-Müller Museum, Otterlo, Holland; the National Museums of Modern Art in Tokyo, Kyoto and Osaka; Yokohama Museum of Art; National Museum of Contemporary Art, Seoul; Hiroshima City Museum of Contemporary Art

관련 동영상

위 기사에서 언급된 그림을 발견한 Emmanuel Layan이 소개하는 Lee Ufan의 작품세계.

source: https://youtu.be/sfz_cScO72E, length: 6:25, caption provided

해외 비평가들이 바라보는 이우환의 작품세계

There is a clear antihumanist thread that runs through both his paintings and installations—an eco-aesthetic critique of how manmade forces gradually violate the natural world, deforming our shared environment. At the same time, one detects a socially engaged concern with the often unseen forces of power exerted upon us in everyday life, manipulating, objectifying and even dehumanizing us as a result. — www.artreview.com

Exhibiting a distilled visual language based on an **amalgamation** of Eastern and Western aesthetics and philosophy, his works emphasize system, structure, and process through fields of dots or lines to create tension between his gestures and the **picture plane**, while marking the passage of time. — www.pacegallery.com

Rather than attempting to shape the world and its varied discourses through his painting and sculpture, he works towards establishing a connection with them. Lee's works do not attempt to forge a conclusion, what matters is the ongoing dialogue. — www. artasiapacific.com

As a painter, he is known for works of almost maximal minimalism: for instance, a series of large canvases, each painted over the course of several weeks, each consisting of one or two intentionally confined brush strokes. He paints with a long broom-like brush, holding his breath for the duration of the brush's movement. Think of him as the pen-like instrument that draws out an earthquake's tremors on a **seismograph**; each of his concise brush strokes reports on the vibrations of the world. — www.wsj.com

* amalgamation: 융합(=mixture, integration), 합병
* picture plane: 화면(畫面)
* seismograph: 지진계

1. 괄호 안 단어를 활용하여 적절한 표현으로 빈 칸을 채워봅시다.

I've always been suspicious of any proposal to build a museum for my work, because a "museum" is fully charged with the __________ (preconceive) idea as a privileged establishment. I am against the notion of the museum as a place for artworks to be presented and appreciated. Whether painting or sculpture, my work is meant to incorporate its __________ (surround) space. Therefore, I don't want my work to look like an independent artwork in a gallery. This is why I was initially against idea of [Lee Ufan Musuem in] Naoshima, but the architect, Tadao Ando, persuaded me by __________ (emphasize) that he would create a "space" for my work, instead of a "museum," although it __________ (official) became a "museum."

2. Lee Ufan의 작품과 제목을 연결시켜 봅시다.

• From Point, 1976 • Dialogue, 2019 • With Winds, 1983 • From Line, 1976

a.

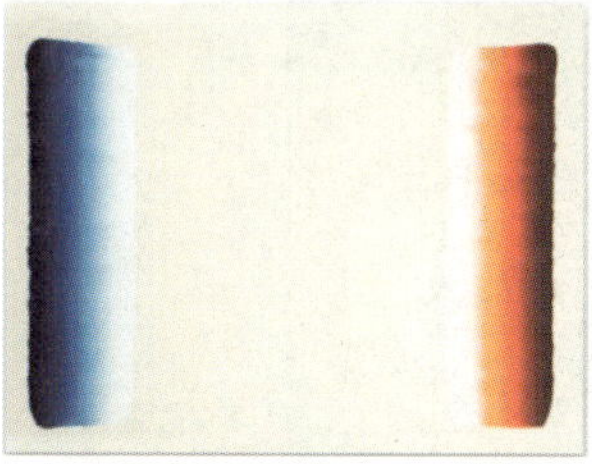

source: www.lissongallery.com

b.

source: www.kamelmennour.com

c.

source: www.moma.org

d.

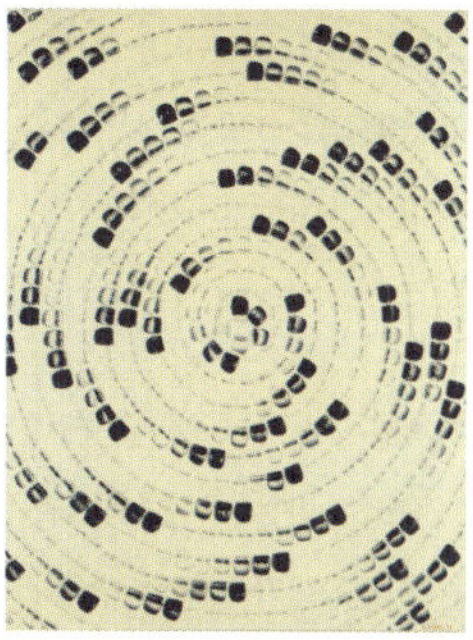

source: www.dailyartfair.com

Do Ho Suh Unveils Architectural Fabric Works at Lehmann Maupin

London's Lehmann Maupin is currently hosting a dynamic digital exhibition featuring new architectural fabric works by the **acclaimed** Korean sculptor and artist, Do Ho Suh. The **eponymous** presentation features large installations of ghost-like rooms and small-scale pieces of domestic objects such as light fixtures and nostalgic devices that explore the concept of space and home.

The virtual presentation offers a brief overview of the artist's groundbreaking approach. "Throughout his career, Suh has investigated the ways in which we occupy and inhabit both public and private space, drawing attention to questions of identity and the role of the individual in today's increasingly global society," said the gallery in a statement.

source: www.designboom.com

Now based in London, Suh continues to elevate his interdisciplinary practice that not only emphasize the **malleability** of space, but also confront issues of cultural identity, memory and marginality.

* acclaimed: 호평 받은(=publically praised as excellent)
* eponymous: 작가 이름과 동일한. 즉 전시명이 Do Ho Suh. Lehmann Maupin에서 2020. 12. 3. ~ 2021. 2. 20. 까지 digitally exhibited.
* malleability: 유연성(=plasticity)

Oftentimes, the pieces he creates are autobiographical. One of his earliest and most widely-recognized pieces entitled *Home Within Home Within Home Within Home* was a silk replica of his first solo home in Rhode Island. The work measured a **staggering** 12 by 15 meters.

* staggering: 믿기 어려운(=astounding), 압도적인(=overwhelming), 충격적인

서도호(Suh Do Ho)

source: www.medium.com

- sculptor and installation artist born in 1962
- renowned for one-to-one scale fabric replicas of his former residences and domestic settings which have notions of time, memory, and identity
- major exhibitions: Whitney Museum of American Art at Philip Morris (2001); Serpentine Gallery, London (2002); Seattle Art Museum (2011); Smithsonian American Art Museum, D.C. (2018); Los Angeles County Museum of Art (2019-2020); Victoria and Albert Museum in London, (2019)
- collections: MOMA, New York; Guggenheim Museum, New York; Museum of Fine Arts, Houston; Museum of Contemporary Art, Los Angeles; Art Gallery of Ontario, Toronto; Tate Modern, London; the Museum of Contemporary Art, Tokyo

해외 비평가들이 바라보는 서도호의 작품세계

The idea of home has long guided Do Ho Suh's artwork. In his eye, a space is never really just a space. Its soul lives within its walls and history. And in return, the space becomes part of those who live there. The memories created, and later revised, are as vivid and real as the places themselves. — www.crfashionbook.com

Best known for his intricate sculptures that defy conventional notions of scale and **site-specificity**, Suh draws attention to the ways viewers occupy and inhabit public space. In several of the artist's floor sculptures, viewers are encouraged to walk on surfaces composed of thousands of miniature human figures. — www.art21.org

Some of his most well-known pieces are his life-size recreations of past residences that have ranged from his traditional Korean-style family home in Seoul and a three-story town house in Providence, Rhode Island, to a brownstone in New York's Chelsea neighborhood. In such works, he meticulously reproduces architectural features and appliances with sheer fabric that visitors can enter and navigate through. — www.artasiapacific.com

His works transform the familiarity of a domestic space into a **liminal** one, where 'home' is both an idealized concept and physical reality. Through these spaces, Suh examines how home and identity are ever-evolving concepts in today's global society, and how culture, tradition, migration, and displacement intersect as we construct our ideas of selfhood and origin. — www.americanart.si.edu

* site-specificity: 장소 특정성. 한 예술 작품이 특정한 장소만을 위해서 만들어진 것을 뜻함. 서도호의 작품은 규모가 크지만 장소를 옮겨 다니면서 전시 가능한 특징을 지님.
* liminal: 한계의, 경계의(=intermediate between two states, conditions, or regions). 작가는 집이라는 친숙한 공간을 이상적인 개념과 물리적 실체의 경계에 있는 곳으로 표현함.

Installation Art (설치 미술) 관련 terminology

conceptual art	심미적인 측면보다 관념이나 아이디어에 중점을 둔 설치 작품	Life Cube Project	지역사회 관객들이 자신의 희망사항을 글로 쓰거나 그리도록 cube 형태의 작품을 설치
Dia Plage	대규모 합성 사진 설치 작품	mural	벽화
earthworks/ land art	땅, 바다 등에 대규모로 설치한 작품	plop art	대형건물, 공원, 공공 건축물 앞에 설치된 공공 작품이 매력적이지 못함을 비하할 때 쓰는 표현
environmental sculpture	관객을 위해 기존의 환경을 바꾸거나 새롭게 창조한 조각 작품	public art	모든 대중들이 시각적 물리적으로 접할 수 있는 작품
found object	상상 하지도 못했던 재료로 만든 작품 (예, Duchamp의 변기)	rock balancing	돌을 쌓아 작품을 제작하는 것
Gesamtkunstwerk	관객들이 모든 감각 기관을 동원하여 감상하도록 고안한 작품	site-specific art	특정 장소에 설치하기 위해 제작한 작품
kinetic art	관객의 움직임을 감지하여 구현되는 작품	sustainable art	생태계, 사회정의, 비폭력의 주제 구현 작품

Rubber Duck by Florentijn Hofman. Source: www.atlasobscura.com

The Koreans at the Top of the Art World

Next week, when V.I.P.s and special guests shuffle through Christie's new West Galleries, in Rockefeller Center, they will **alight on** a series of abstract paintings by a group of relatively unknown artists. These pieces reflect a recent market craze for attractive work with an emphasis on process and materials. But the artists at the West Galleries are not young painters from Brooklyn, Berlin, or Los Angeles. They are a group of Korean **octogenarians** who comprise a movement known as Tansaekhwa (or "Dansaekhwa") and have been producing in this style since the nineteen-seventies.

source: www.koreasociety.org

Tansaekhwa will receive the red-carpet treatment from Christie's, with a **sumptuous** 136-page catalogue and prices to match: a million dollars for a work by Park Seo-Bo, $1.5 million for a Chung Sang-Hwa. By the standards of today's **frothy** art market, the prices are far from eye-watering, but for the artists, who until now were mostly forgotten even within Korea, they are almost **unfathomable**. "I am unbelievably happy," the artist Ha Chong-Hyun said on the phone from Korea. "I'm eighty-one years old. Back in the day, Koreans didn't live this long. I shouldn't be here. But to have this happen in my lifetime, I can't be more thankful."

* alight on: 우연히 마주하다(=find or meet by chance)
* octogenarian: 나이가 80대인 사람(=a person between 80 and 90 years of age)
* sumptuous: 호화로운(=lavish)
* frothy: 거품 많은(=foamy, bubbly)
* unfathomable: 이해할 수 없는(=inexplicable, baffling)

After four decades of **languishing**, with occasional exhibitions in regional galleries around Korea and Japan, Ha has, within the last year, landed his first solo show in New York, seen his work enter the Museum of Modern Art's permanent collection, attended the opening of a highly **lauded** Tansaekhwa show in Venice, and watched forty-five of his paintings go on the auction block, with nine selling for more than a hundred thousand dollars. Prior to 2014, his auction record was a mere $13,303, and, in the six years from 2007 through 2013, when eight works of his went to auction, half went unsold. "To be honest, it was not possible to make a living making this kind of work in Korea," Ha said. "I was so tired and it's such welcome news."

* languishing: 활기가 없음
* lauded: 찬사를 받는(=praised, extolled)

Focus on Grammar

◈ 소유대명사

Prior to 2014, his auction record was a mere $13,303, and, in the six years from 2007 through 2013, when eight works of *his* went to auction, half went unsold.

소유대명사(possessive pronoun)는 소유격 형용사와 명사를 합친 것으로, 명사구 전체의 반복을 피할 때 사용한다; 예, Whose coat is this? Is this yours(←your coat)? 또한 위의 예시문처럼 '한정사+핵심명사+of+possessive pronoun'의 구문에서도 많이 사용된다. 위 문장의 'eight works of his'는 'his eight works'로 바꿀 수 있다. 하지만 이러한 변환이 모든 경우에 가능하지는 않다. 'She was moving out and she gave the dishes and bowls to some friends of hers' 문장의 경우 '... the dishes and bowls to her some friends'로 변환할 수 없다. 한정사에는 여러 세부 종류가 있는데 그들 사이에는 사용의 순서가 있으며, 한 위치에는 하나의 한정사만 사용이 가능하다. 그런데 her와 some은 같은 위치에 사용이 되므로 둘 중 하나만 가능하다. 이를 상보적 분포(complementary distribution)라고 부른다.

Although he was the dean at Korea's most prestigious art school, Hongik University, for many years, Park Seo-Bo, who is eighty-four, had a negligible market as well. Park's 1982 piece "**Ecriture** 3-82" was sold in November, 2013, for $56,750 and then resold in May of this year for $631,972. In the nineteen-eighties, Park said, he couldn't sell this kind of work for even three million Korean won, which, at the time, was equivalent to less than four thousand dollars.

Ecriture 3-82
source: www.mutualart.com

This sudden attention has **blindsided** the Tansaekhwa artists, but it coincides with a new global focus in the art world. Galleries are opening **outposts**; collectors from emerging economies are increasing their influence; and museums are revising the art-historical narrative to include under-recognized artists and movements. Tansaekhwa has found itself at the nexus of a number of changes. Alexandra Munroe, the curator of the 2011 Guggenheim Museum retrospective of Lee Ufan, an artist associated with Tansaekhwa and its most prominent **exponent**, describes it as a "perfect storm."

* ecriture: 묘법(描法, 점이나 선으로 사물을 묘사하는 방법)
* blindside: 놀라게 하다, 곤혹스럽게 하다
* exponent: 대표적 인물(=representative)

"Focus on Vocabulary"

◈ **outpost:** 군대의 전초 부대에 비유하여 지점(支店)을 의미

원래는 군대에서 주로 쓰이던 용어인데 일상에서 비유적 의미로 자주 사용되는 단어들 중 무기와 관련된 표현들을 살펴보면,

barrage	연속적 포격 → 질문 공세, 정보의 홍수	high-caliber	총기의 구경이 큰 → 고품질, 뛰어난 역량
big gun	파괴력이 큰 무기 → 중요 인사	shrapnel	파편 → 잔돈(small change)
bombshell	포탄 → 충격적인 소식	snipe	저격하다 → 비난하다

The powerful art adviser Allan Schwartzman, who has taken a keen interest in Tansaekhwa, said, "I've never seen this amount of widening interest in a particular circle of non-contemporary artists, in historical material before." The number of upcoming exhibitions associated with the group this fall supports Schwartzman's observation.

In New York alone, the blue-chip galleries Blum & Poe, Galerie Perrotin, and Tina Kim will open shows of Yun Hyong-Keun, Chung Chang-Sup, and Ha Chong-Hyun respectively, within a week of each other, starting on October 30th. In London during **Frieze Week**, in mid-October, no fewer than three exhibitors—Axel Vervoordt, Kukje Gallery/Tina Kim, and Hakgojae—will be showing Tansaekhwa works at **Frieze Masters**. South of the fair, in a **tony** gallery space next to the Royal Academy of Art, the global mega gallery Pace will host a retrospective of Lee Ufan's paintings from the Tansaekhwa period.

* tony: 멋진(=stylish), 세련된

Focus on Terminology

◆ Frieze Week

Frieze Week는 Frieze 회사에서 주최하는 일주일 동안의 다양한 현대 예술 전시 기간으로 London, New York, Los Angeles에서 펼쳐진다. 행사 기간은 지역마다 다르다. 미술관, 박물관, 공공 기관 등 다양한 장소에서 전시회를 개최하며 그 외 수많은 이벤트들이 진행된다.

source: www.artsharesales.com

◆ Frieze Masters

Frieze Masters는 Frieze Week in London (Frieze London)의 전시 행사 중 하나로 과거와 현재 예술의 관계를 살펴볼 기회를 제공하고자 기획된 것이다. Frieze London의 행사장 바로 인근에서 진행되는데, Frieze London이 2000년 이후의 작품을 주로 전시하는 반면에 Frieze Masters는 2000년 이전의 작품을 소개한다.

What started the market phenomenon? It can be traced to two shows of major historical works: one, at Kukje Gallery in Seoul, in August, 2014, and, less than a month later, a show at Blum & Poe in Los Angeles, which was curated by Joan Kee, an art historian who authored "Contemporary Korean Art: Tansaekhwa and the Urgency of Method," the first book on the movement in English.

source: www.amazon.com

The artists credit her for spurring international interest in their work. Following the two exhibitions, a number of institutions acquired Tansaekhwa works, including the Art Institute of Chicago; the Centre Pompidou, in Paris; the Guggenheim Museum in New York and Abu Dhabi; the Hirshhorn Museum, in Washington, D.C.; the Museum of Modern Art, in New York; and M+ in Hong Kong. Important American collectors, such as Howard Rachofsky, who, with his wife, Cindy, has promised their entire collection to the Dallas Museum of Art, also bought from these shows, under Schwartzman's guidance.

As collectors took their cue from these influential tastemakers, auction prices went up. Since the Blum & Poe and Kukje shows last year, seventy-two works by Chung Sang-Hwa, Park Seo-Bo, Ha Chong-Hyun, and Yun Hyong-Keun have sold for more than a hundred thousand dollars each at auction. Prior to that, only four works had surpassed a hundred thousand dollars, ever. Although the sales took place in Asia, more than half of the bidders were Western collectors and new clients, Jihyun Lee, a specialist at K Auction, which holds auctions in Korea and Hong Kong, said. Seoul-based Yunah Jung, who is organizing the Christie's selling exhibition, **concurs** that Western interest is driving the market.

* concur: 동의하다

Joan Kee, the art historian, says that Tansaekhwa has that "extra **oomph** factor" from its association to Lee Ufan, who was acclaimed in the late nineteen-sixties as the main theorist behind the Japanese postwar movement **Mono-ha**. But she cautions that Tansaekhwa was not an official movement; there was no **manifesto**, nor a clearly defined group of members. The term, meaning, literally, "monochrome painting," appeared in the mid-nineteen-seventies to describe an innovative approach to process, which differed from artist to artist. Lee Ufan created works consisting of lines, made by dragging his brush down the length of the canvas until the **pigment** disappeared, and points, made by repeatedly pressing the tip of the brush against the canvas until the paint was used up. Park Seo-Bo used pencil to draw dense scribbles, **wispy** lines, and **sinuous** loops into the still-wet surface of the painted canvas. Chung Sang-Hwa covered the canvas in a layer of zinc-based paint, laboriously stripped away sections and then repainted those areas with a slightly glossier acrylic paint.

* oomph: 매력
* manifesto: 선언문(=a public declaration of principles or intentions)
* pigment: 안료(=substance used as coloring)
* wispy: (촘촘하지 않은) 몇 가닥의
* sinuous: 물결모양의, 구불구불한

"Focus on Terminology"

◆ Mono-ha

Mono-ha (School of Things, 物派)는 1960년대 중반 도쿄에서 탄생한 예술 운동이다. 참여한 예술가들은 돌, 흙, 나무, 면, 종이, 철판, 유리, 파라핀 같은 자연과 산업 현장에서 볼 수 있는 사물들—things (mono)—을 그 자체 또는 서로 조합하여 제시하였다. Mono-ha는 사물들을 그들의 원초적인 형태로 축소함으로써 작품을 형상화하고자 했다. 사물들의 형태를 변화시키지 않으며 또한 재료로 여기지 않고, 사물들 그 자체가 의미를 지니고 있으며 자율적인 것으로 바라보았다. Mono-ha의 선두적인 작가로 이우환(Lee Ufan)과 Nobuo Sekine(關根 伸夫)를 꼽을 수 있는데 그들은 작가의 창조적 능력이 기술에 의해서 무력화되고 있음을 인식하고 인위적으로 무엇인가를 만드는 것을 반대하였다.

단색화 화가들의 작품

Untitled 78-11-29

by Chung Sang-Hwa
사진 김경석

Ecriture 170225

by Park Seo-Bo
www.ravoux.co.kr

Conjunction 74-98

by Ha Chong-Hyun
사진 김경석

Untitled

by Yun Hyong-Keun
www.brooklynrail.org

As the big galleries become bigger, through larger spaces and multiple locations in cities around the world, and as the proliferation of art fairs continues **unabated**, more programming is needed than ever before. Tansaekhwa is particularly appealing, because, in addition to their considerable inventories of historical material, most of the artists continue to make new work. Plus, their **oeuvre** is almost exclusively painting, which remains the market's most saleable medium. "Painting is painting," the dealer Tim Blum said. "It's a kind of a **no-brainer** in terms of how that gets marketed, collected and contextualized."

Despite numerous institutional acquisitions, Tansaekhwa has yet to receive a major museum show, and the work may soon get too expensive for continued museum interest. "When you jump from two hundred thousand dollars to a million dollars, that's going to **kick the museums out of the market**," Schwartzman said, adding that, with the new price levels, "Markets always have a certain plateau level. It needs a next group of collectors."

* unabated: 줄지 않는, 약해지지 않는
* oeuvre: 모든 작품
* no-brainer: 쉬운 일(=anything requiring little thought or effort)

"Focus on Vocabulary"

◈ kick something out of the market

When you jump from two hundred thousand dollars to a million dollars, that's going to *kick the museums out of the market*.

'kick something out of somewhere'는 '~을 어디에서 내쫒는다'는 뜻을 지니고 있다. 위 문장에서는 작품의 가치가 $200,000에서 $1,000,000로 오르게 되면 museum을 통한 거래는 더 이상 이루어지지 않고 (고가의 미술품을 거래하는) 경매장 같은 곳에서 거래가 이루어질 거라는 의미를 내포하고 있다.

작품을 설명할 때 사용하는 abbreviations

ac or a/c	artist's copy
a/f or a.f.	as found
ap or a/p	artist's proof
b.	born
bat or b.a.t.	Bon A Tirer (final print proof)
C	century
c. or cir.	circa 대략, ... 경
chk.	chalk
chl.	charcoal
col	color
c/w	comes (combined, complete, or coupled) with
d.	dated
del. or delt.	s/he drew (it)
dr	drawing
ed. or edn.	edition of
est.	estimate
exec.	executed
exh. or exhib.	exhibited
F&G	framed and glazed 액자에 넣고 유리를 끼운
f. or fecit	s/he made (it)
fl. or floruit	flourished
h.c.	hors commerce (not for sale)
htd	heightened
i.	inscribed 쓰여진
imp.	s/he printed (it)
inc.	engraved it 새기다
inits.	initials
inv. or invenit	s/he invented (it)
jnr.	junior
lit.	literature

lith.or lithog.	lithograph 석판인쇄
mono.	monogram
n.d. or N.D.	no date, not dated
n.p. or N.P.	no publisher
num.	number
o/c	oil on canvas
pa or p/a	artist's proof
pinx. or pxt. or pinxt. or pinxit	s/he painted (it)
pl	plate
pp	printer's proof
prov.	provenance 출처
/R	illustrated in sale catalogue
rec.	rectangular
recto	the front side of a picture
rem.	remains of
s.	signed
sc. or sct. or sculp. or sculpt or sculpsit	s/he engraved, carved, or sculptured (it)
sig.	signature
s/n	signed and numbered
snr.	senior
st.	stamped
verso	reverse side, or back, of a picture
w/c	watercolor
?	unknown dimensions, date or nationality, or illegible initial(s) or letter(s)

Two Landmark US Museum Shows Will Spotlight the Long Overlooked History of Modern and Avant-Garde Korean Art

The story of 20th-century Korean art is woefully underrepresented to many students of Western art history. But in the coming years, a pair of shows at institutions on **either side of the US** will aim to correct that. Coming to the Los Angeles County Museum of Art in 2022 is an ambitious survey of modern Korean painting, photography, and sculpture from 1897 to 1965.

The show, organized by LACMA's associate curator of Korean art, Virginia Moon, spans two eras of Korean history—**the last gasp** of the Joseon dynasty, which lasted over 500 years, until the birth of the independent Korean nation in 1910; and the contemporary era, which includes the period in which Korea split into two **sovereign** states. "This 'space between' the traditional and contemporary is one of the most revealing time periods in Korean history given the historic event... as the country 'reluctantly' modernized during this time," Moon tells Artnet News.

* either side of the US: 미국의 동·서부
* the last gasp: 마지막 순간

"Focus on Terminology"

◈ sovereign, 명사/형용사

1. 명사: 군주, 국왕(=a person exercising supreme authority usually by hereditary right)
2. 형용사: 자주의, 독립의, 주권을 지닌

◈ sovereign wealth fund (SWF)

'국부펀드'라 부르는 시사경제용어. 국가가 외환보유고 같은 자산을 운용하기 위해 설립한 특별 투자펀드로 투자대상은 외국의 국채나 회사채에서부터 금융회사, 에너지회사, 항만, 통신, 원자재, 사모펀드 등으로 다양하다. 국부펀드는 정부가 소유한 돈으로 운용실태나 실적 등이 대부분 비밀에 가려져 있다.

Some 140 works of art are expected to be in the show, a selection that includes examples of early 20th-century sculpture and photography that have rarely been shown outside of the country. "It was important to show how the two periods—modern and contemporary—connected, how these different media first appeared in Korea, and how, over time, the modern led to the now," Moon adds. "The modern art period in Korea, unknown in the US until now, is evidence that contemporary art in Korea did not suddenly appear out of a **void**."

The exhibition is the second of three shows introducing Korean arts to American audiences. The first of the bunch, a historical presentation of Korean writing and calligraphy practices, took place at the museum last year. The third exhibition will take place in 2025.

Meanwhile, in the spring of 2022, the Guggenheim in New York will present "The Avant-Garde: Experimental Art in South Korea, in 1960s-1970s." The museum calls it the first exhibition in North America to explore the wave of experimentalist artists that rose to prominence in the decades following the Korean War of the early 1950s, such as Lee Kang-so, Lee Kun-yong, and Lee Seung-taek.

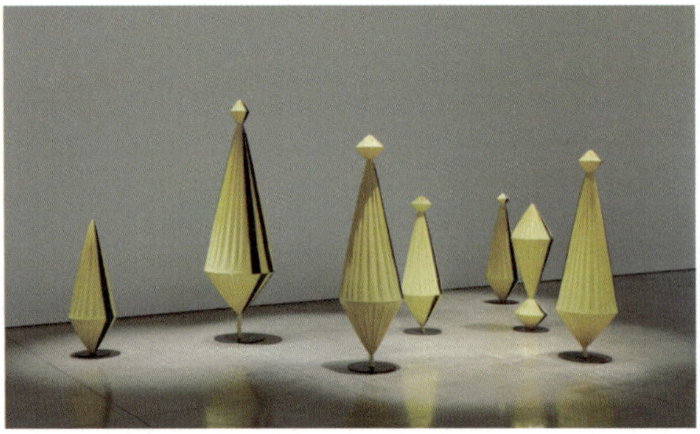

Untitled by Lee Seung-taek
source: www.dailyartfair.com

* void: 공간(=empty space), 무(無)

◇ 다음 단어와 같은 의미를 지닌 단어를 위 글에서 찾아봅시다.

1. proof	2. distinction	3. assortment
4. trial (a.)	5. cluster	6. research (v.)

"Spanning the 1960s and the 1970s, this upcoming presentation examines a group of loosely affiliated artists whose artistic production reflected and responded to the rapidly changing and globalizing socio-political and material conditions that shaped South Korea," a representative from the museum says of the show. "It reveals the innovative approach to art-making by a remarkable generation of Korean artists and features **seminal** works in painting, sculpture, installation, performance, photography, and film."

The exhibition was co-organized by Kyung An, an assistant curator of Asian Art at the Guggenheim, and Soojung Kang, a senior curator at the National Museum of Modern and Contemporary Art, Korea. It will be presented **in tandem** at both institutions.

* seminal: 독창적인(=highly original)
* in tandem: 협력하여(=in conjunction)

Los Angeles County Museum of Art

source: www.gagosian.com

Guggenheim, New York

source: www.mymodernmet.com

< Famous Quotes About Painting >

- A work of art which did not begin in emotion is not art. — Paul Cezanne
- Art is a line around your thoughts. — Gustav Klimt
- As I work at my drawings, day after day, what seemed unattainable before is now gradually becoming possible. Slowly, I'm learning to observe and measure. I don't stand quite so helpless before nature any longer. — Vincent van Gogh
- There is no must in art because art is free. — Wassily Kandinsky
- A true artist is not one who is inspired, but one who inspires others. — Salvador Dali
- In drawing, one must look for or suspect that there is more than is casually seen. — George Bridgman
- If I create from the heart, nearly everything works; if from the head, almost nothing. — Marc Chagall
- When I paint, I never think of selling. People fail to understand that we paint in order to experiment and to develop ourselves as we strive for greater heights. — Edvard Munch
- Drawing is not what one sees, but what one can make others see. — Edgar Degas
- More important than a work of art itself is what it will sow. Art can die, a painting can disappear. What counts is the seed. — Joan Miro
- Drawing is still basically the same as it has been since prehistoric times. It brings together man and the world. It lives through magic. — Keith Haring
- Drawing makes you see things clearer, and clearer and clearer still, until your eyes ache. — David Hockney
- If you could say it in words, there would be no reason to paint. — Edward Hopper
- What keeps my heart awake is colorful silence. — Claude Monet
- I am not sick. I am broken. But I am happy to be alive as long as I can paint. — Frida Kahlo

Cross-word Puzzle

ACROSS

3. to have the same opinion
8. to come by chance
11. filled with bubbles
15. tending to overwhelm
6. lack of vitality
10. stylish or distinctive
13. the state of being flexible
16. splendid and expensive-looking

DOWN

1. moving in a curving way
4. the quality of being attractive
7. between two different states
12. to surprise someone
2. publicly acknowledged as excellent
5. combining into an integral whole
9. named after its creator
14. a person who is a symbol

Answer Key

p. 10
1. involved
2. memory
3. particular
4. supply
5. taste

p. 11
1. offshoot
2. overwhelming
3. vocabulary
4. solidified
5. uptick
6. hosts

p. 14
1. slated
   beloved
   abilities
   adaptation
   sizzling
   delight
2. a. soaring
   b. dropped
   c. exploring
   d. cast

p. 19
1. spiced
2. chemistry
3. immune
4. treat
5. unfortunately
6. worth

p. 21
1. acquired
   arm
   acclaimed
   meaning
   expand
   synergy
2. a. released
   b. was
   c. has had
   d. becoming
   e. be seen

p. 26
1. everyday
   spared
   benchmarked
   emotional
   longevity
   expressed
2. a. was
   b. is interlinked
   c. tending
   d. worse
   e. starvation

p. 31
1. company
   cast
   ailing
   temp
   astounding
   drag
2. a. gaining
   b. financial
   c. restrained
   d. assured

p. 32
낭만닥터 김사부
피고인

슬기로운 감방생활
백일의 낭군님
동백꽃 필 무렵
열혈사제
사이코지만 괜찮아
부부의 세계
모범택시
Good Manager
Fight for My Way
Romance is a Bonus Book
The Crowned Clown
Hospital Playlist
SKY Castle
Mr. Queen
The Uncanny Counter
Hometown Cha-Cha-Cha

p. 34
Across
2. snazzy
4. buffer
5. inept
7. protagonist
10. instill
11. dormant
14. plague
15. trope
Down
1. burgeon
2. sprint
3. affliction
6. uptick
8. wallow
9. shady
12. ravage
13. gush

p. 42
1. eschew
2. pride
3. unprecedented
4. drive
5. strain
6. intrusion
7. relentless

p. 44
1. envoy
conferred
assignment
accompany
attend
adopted
2. a. exhibiting
b. called
c. individuality
d. exploitation
e. is regarded

p. 45
1. limit
2. locally
3. temporarily
4. violate
5. altogether
6. fear

p. 58
1. attended
respectively
staged
stunned
accessorize
complete
tied
2. a. flaming
b. lit
c. paired

p. 65
Across
2. emulate
5. protocol
6. flair

8. beguiling
10. adroitly
11. glitz
12. snippet
15. thorny
Down
1. stardust
3. spawn
4. prosaic
7. coveted
8. burnish
9. gallop
13. eschew
14. frenzy

p. 76
1. loan
2. sardonic
3. empathise
4. charm
5. balance out

p. 83
alike
feeding
lingering
instability
fast-paced
highest
trapped
be ignored
stepping
knowing
rise

p. 84
설국열차
국제시장
밀정
청년경찰
군함도
완벽한 타인
엑시트
남산의 부장들
승리호
Architecture 101
Miss Granny
A Violent Prosecutor
Confidential Assignment
The Outlaws
Along with the Gods: The Last 49 Days
Extreme Jobs
Time to Hunt
Escape from Mogadishu

p. 87
Across
1. sass
3. harrowing
6. sardonic
8. fester
9. bellwether
11. vie
12. destitute
13. enthrall
15. aficionado
16. banter
Down
2. shark
4. infiltrate
5. unsettling
7. seminal
10. emote
14. redeem

p. 93
released
explosive
marinated
translates
viral
challenge
variations
hit

doubles
portfolio
foray

p. 99
a. 이유
b. 양보
c. 시간
d. 이유
e. 시간
f. 조건

p. 111
a. Samgyeopsal (삼겹살)
b. Jajangmyun (짜장면)
c. Naengmyun (냉면)
d. Samgyetang (삼계탕)
e. Japchae (잡채)
f. Seolleongtang (설렁탕)
g. Soondae (순대)

p. 122
Across
2. dollop
4. earthy
6. cringe
10. afloat
12. audacious
13. geek
14. thrive
15. staple
Down
1. foray
3. meticulous
5. gravitate
7. foodie
8. slick
9. palate
11. tangy
15. soggy

p. 129
1. barrier
2. routine
3. immunity
4. reflection
5. transport
6. soothing

p. 134
1. edge
2. boom
3. destination
4. age
5. share
6. account
7. band

p. 143
adverse
reaction
impervious
buzzing
perennial
options
deserves
routine

p. 145
Across
4. slather
7. hyphenate
8. pack
9. bout
10. exfoliate
14. regenerative
15. unassuming
16. pushback
Down
1. dabble
2. headspace
3. steep
5. oversaturated
6. venom

11. foothold
12. antifungal
13. detoxify

p. 154
1. detailed
2. continue
3. clear
4. marry
5. balanced
6. formal

p. 157
1. historic
   rise
   cements
   forefront
   references
   viral
2. a. be stocked
   b. ostensibly
   c. aesthetic
   d. carries

p. 167
1. degraded
2. deactivate
3. detach
4. deflected
5. defrost

p. 168
1. asset
2. warehouse
3. agency
4. database
5. currency
6. profit

p. 172
target
original
affordable
marketable
allotted
artistic
are hired
experiment
garment
needed
annual
vary

p. 174
Across
3. traction
6. ethereal
8. demographic
11. faux
12. stellar
13. emblazoned
14. wow
Down
1. curated
2. tutelage
4. asymmetrical
5. whimsical
7. vanguard
9. impeccably
10. bustling
12. scoop

p. 179
1. preconceived
   surrounding
   emphasizing
   officially
2. a. Dialogue, 2019
   b. With Winds, 1983
   c. From Line, 1976
   d. From Point, 1976

p. 194

1. evidence
2. prominence
3. selection
4. experimental
5. bunch
6. explore

p. 197

Across

3. concur
6. languishing
8. alight
10. tony
11. frothy
13. malleability
15. staggering
16. sumptuous

Down

1. sinuous
2. acclaimed
4. oomph
5. amalgamation
7. liminal
9. eponymous
12. blindside
14. exponent

Vocabulary Index

audacious
bahn mi
bao
buoyed
connoisseur
consolidate
cringe
cross
culinary
dollop
earthy
efficacy
entity
ethnopharmacology
fan favorite
fermented
fit-out
foodie
foray
ganache
gasp for air
geek
generously
gravitate
guidance necessary
hobble
in a subtle way
in the works
logistics
mainstream
marinate
marry
matcha
meringue
mesmerize
meticulous
pad thai
palate
panna cotta
render
retreat
scallion
self-professed
slick
soggy
spin
staple
street classic
suppress
sweeping
tangy
thrive
turn off
tweak
umami
umeshu
uni
vibrant

K-Beauty

antifungal
anti-inflammation
bout
buzzy
dabble
detoxify
exfoliate
foothold
headspace
houttuynia cordata
hyphenate
in one go
microbiome
mucin
mugwort
oversaturated
pack
pared-back
pushback
range
regenerative
rehmannia
sacred lotus
serein
slather
steep
tier
venom

K-Fashion

archival
asymmetrical
blow away
branded
bubbly
bustling
buzz
calling
capsule
catch on
centric
conducive
cultish
curated
designer label
embellishment
emblazoned
endorse
e-tailer
ethereal
faux
funnel
hype-driven
impeccably
in a similar vein
mainstay
mantra
marry
narrative
niche
on the flip side
organically
peplum dress
scoop up
selvedge
stateside
stellar
stockist
timeless
traction
tutelage
vanguard
whimsical
wonky
wow

K-Arts

acclaimed
alight on
amalgamation
blindside
concur
ecriture
eponymous
exponent
frothy
in tandem
languishing
last gasp
lauded
liminal
malleability
manifesto
no-brainer
octogenarian
oeuvre
oomph
picture plane
pigment
seismograph
seminal
sinuous
site-specificity
staggering
sumptuous
tony
unabated
unfathomable
void
wispy

Credits

text

p. 6-12	adapted from https://www.dw.com/en/korean-tv-dramas-finda-huge-audience-in-india/a-56815880
p. 14	adapted from https://www.thestar.com.my/lifestyle/entertainment/hit-k-drama-crash-landing-on-you-to-return-as-a-musical
p. 15-19	adapted from https://www.cinemaescapist.com/2020/02/review-itaewon-class
p. 21	adapted from www.nme.com/en_asia/itaewon-class-english-remake
p. 22-24	adapted from https://www.thrillist.com/entertainment/nation/netflix-kingdom-review
p. 26	adapted from https://variety.com/2019/artisans/production/netflix-south-korea-zombie-series-kingdom
p. 27-29	adapted from https://www.clickthecity.com/tv/article/78477/k-drama-files-my-mister-and-its-story-of-loneliness/
p. 31	adapted from https://collider.com/best-korean-dramas-on-netflix/
p. 36-43	adapted from https://www.asiamediacentre.org.nz/features/can-south-koreas-pop-superstars-sell-everything/
p. 44	adapted from www.washingtonpost.com/world/2021/09/14/bts-un-assembly/
p. 45-47	adapted from https://variety.com/2021/music/musicians/bts-mcdonalds-meal-indonesia-1234994871/
p. 52-56	adapted from https://people.com/music/blackpink-what-you-need-to-know-about-kpops-biggest-girl-group/
p. 58	adapted from https://hypebae.com/2021/10/blackpink-jennie-chanel-spring-summer-2022-paris-fashion-week-front-row-outfits
p. 59-60	adapted from https://www.nme.com/news/music/ncthollywood-sm-entertainment-us-based-k-pop-tv-competition-series-2935723
p. 62	adapted from https://www.billboard.com/articles/columns/k-town/
p. 68-69	adapted from www.theguardian.com/film/2020/feb/10/parasite-first-foreign-language-film-to-win-best-picture-oscar
p. 71-72	adapted from www.oscars.org
p. 74-77	adapted from https://gulfnews.com/entertainment/hollywood/why-korean-movie-pawn-is-the-perfect-feel-good-film-to-watch-this-week-in-the-uae
p. 80-82	adapted from https://www.oprahdaily.com/entertainment/tv-movies/g37029397/korean-zombie-movies/
p. 83	adapted from https://www.tripzilla.com/korean-zombie-movies-netflix/120800
p. 90-91	adapted from https://abcnews.go.com/International/foodies-globe-taking-part-fire-noodle-challenge/story?id=59594235
p. 93	adapted from https://www.straitstimes.com/asia/east-asia
p. 95-98	adapted from https://www.thechronicleherald.ca/news/local/
p. 101-105	adapted from https://www.mensjournal.com/food-drink/kimchi-is-giving-classic-american-food-a-new-kick
p. 107-110	adapted from https://dc.eater.com/2020/11/13/21563899/bangbop-opening-delivery-brookland
p. 115-117	adapted from https://www.broadsheet.com.au/adelaide/food-and-drink/article/now-open-get-croiffles-croissant-waffle-hybrid-and-dalgona-coffees-seoul-sweetie-new-korean-dessert-bar-adelaides-cbd
p. 118-120	adapted from https://www.express.co.uk/life-style/health/1305870/how-to-get-to-sleep-better-improve-ginseng-extract
p. 124-130	adapted from https://www.vogue.com/article/k-beautytrendsto-try-in-2021
p. 133-136	adapted from https://asia.nikkei.com/Business/Consumer/K-beauty-comes-to-Turkey-as-Korean-cosmetics-exports-boom
p. 138-140	adapted from https://timesofindia.indiatimes.com/life-style/beauty/k-beauty-regimes-are-ruling-india-claims-study-data/articleshow/85451542.cms
p. 143	adapted from www.timesnownews.com
p. 148-154	adapted from https://www.scmp.com/magazines/style/celebrity/article/3082580/5-emerging-korean-designer-labels-driving-k-fashions
p. 157	adapted from https://www.elle.com/fashion/a37213015/best-korean-fashion-brands/

p. 158-163 adapted from https://hypebeast.com/2020/10/korean-fashionbrands-london-ujng-xu-store-emerging-designers

p. 164 adapted from https://www.reddit.com

p. 165-170 adapted from https://www.glossy.co/fashion/k-fashion/

p. 172 adapted from https://work.chron.com/careers-textile-industry-10262.html

p. 176 adapted from https://tntribune.com/video-frame-at-last-masters-lost-painting-missing-for-45-years-up-for-sale-at-850000/

p. 179 adapted from https://www.artforum.com/interviews/lee-ufan-discusses-space

p. 180-181 adapted from https://hypebeast.com/2021/1/do-ho-suh-exhibition-lehmann-maupin-exhibition

p. 184-191 adapted from https://www.newyorker.com/culture/culture-desk/the-koreans-at-the-top-of-the-art-world

p. 193-195 adapted from https://news.artnet.com/art-world/modern-avant-garde-korean-art-north-america-1922473